USN

NAVAL OPERATIONS IN THE '80s
USN
MICHAEL SKINNER

★
PRESIDIO

Dedication:

To George Hall
and Michael Whitten
and all the boys of Hobby Night
all around the world.

Published by Presidio Press, 31 Pamaron Way, Novato, CA 94947

Library of Congress Cataloging in Publication Data

Skinner, Michael, 1953-
U S N, naval operations in the 80s.

(Presidio seapower series)
1. United States. Navy—History—20th century.
I. Title.   II. Title: USN, naval operations in the 80s.   III. Series.
VA58.4.S48   1986   359'.00973   85-30140
ISBN 0-89141-209-3

Printed in Japan by
Dai Nippon Printing Co., Ltd.

Half-title: "Big John," *(John F. Kennedy, CV-67)*

Title: Guided missile cruiser *England* fires a Standard surface-to-air missile. *Photo courtesy FMC.*

This page: Haddock, *Permit*-class nuclear submarine, comes under the Golden Gate Bridge.

Contents

621

The *Enterprise.*

Preface

The USN is a particularly *American* navy. They have their own style, go their own way. No other navy in the world, for example, operates a super-carrier. But big-deck, nuclear-powered carrier fever, along with a similar, unproven faith in nuclear-powered fast attack submarines, dominate American naval thinking.

It's always been that way. The United States Navy has a history of audacious acts. Years before there *was* a Navy Department, years before the new country had proper warships, the colonists twisted the tail of the British lion at sea. The feat was repeated in the War of 1812. America had seventeen ships, the British more than six hundred. But the U.S. won that war, as well.

In fact, the USN has never lost a war at sea. They kept the sea lanes open and the supplies flowing in both world wars, and thrashed the Japanese in the Pacific in an almost unilateral campaign. In Korea, in Vietnam, in hundreds of hotspots since, America's response to crisis has been a *naval* response.

But there's new trouble on the horizon for the American Navy. If the USN is following a different drummer, the Soviet Union steps to the beat of navy marches of the past. As one defense analyst put it, the Russians are hoping to win the next war with the tactics that lost the last one: the Nazi wolfpack concept and Japanese-style kamikaze attacks. Whether or not these concepts can succeed by substituting nuclear attack submarines for U-boats and cruise missiles for kamikaze planes depends on whom you talk with. We'll discuss what the experts are saying. But it's to be hoped that we'll never find out for sure.

The next war at sea holds the potential of great destruction, even without the use of nuclear weapons. I say "potential" because there are a number of scenarios that can be postulated, from an all out, bloody slugfest to a "phony war" in viii

which both sides stay out of one another's way, waiting for an elusive tactical advantage.

Losing means utter destruction. The winner will not be much better off. Ships will run though ammunition at an alarming rate. It could be that the side with the last missile will win the war. The aspects of naval warfare that get the least attention in peacetime—logistics, damage control, training—will be the deciding factors in wartime. Weapons alone are not enough. There are going to be a lot of shiny new ships at the bottom of the ocean at the end of the next war.

This book kicks off the Presidio Seapower series. It is meant to be an overview, an introduction to naval operations and the current issues under debate in the naval world. As such, it is necessarily sketchy at times. Whole books have been written just on naval guns, for example. Later books in the series will cover naval topics in greater depth.

Some subjects have already been tackled. For example, *CV: Carrier Aviation* neatly bridges the gap between Presidio's Seapower and Airpower series. Carriers are also covered in *USN*, of course, but this book concentrates on the ships rather than the planes.

Good Navy data is hard to find. The Navy itself is not that forthcoming, and most of the published material just repeats earlier, often incorrect, reports. There are only a few people doing original work on naval matters in this country, starting with the "two Normans," Norman Polmar and Norman Friedman. Jan S. Breemer's *U.S. Naval Developments* was also helpful, as was the U.S.

Naval Institute's *Bluejackets Manual.* Of course, no one can write anything about the Navy without first consulting the Institute's *Proceedings,* the monthly bible of the American naval community. *The Hook* is a similar publication that deals with the world of carrier aviation.

A word of caution: I have never been on a Soviet warship, nor have I been in the combat information center (CIC) of a ship in action, though I write about both topics in detail. Every effort has been made to be as accurate as possible, both in fact and tone, but some things can be known only first hand. Valuable insight was provided by manuscript readers Capt. Richard Phohli, USN Retired, Lt. Mark Nicholson, USNR, and Alan Toon. Still, any errors remaining are my responsibility, and I want to know about them. *USN* will be periodically updated, and any corrections, clarifications, or additions are cheerfully welcomed.

Many thanks this time around to Tom Hall of the Navy's Recruiting Command, Bob Suarez, editor of *Raytheon Magazine* (where some portions of Chapters 3 and 4 first appeared), and the Kaypro Corporation. Thanks also to the officers and men of the U.S.S. *America,* U.S.S. *Barry,* and U.S.S. *Lexington* for their kind assistance, as well as all those crewmen, ashore and at sea, admirals and deck apes, who took the time to try to explain what it's like to spend a life on the Great Ocean.

Michael Skinner
Atlanta, 1986

Handler—Crewman involved with spotting and moving aircraft; also called "mangler"

Hangar Deck—Area underneath flight deck where aircraft are maintained and stored

Harpoon—RGM-84; USN medium-range cruise missile

Hawkeye—E-2C radar aircraft: the "Hummer" or "Frisbee"

Helmsman—Crewman in charge of steering a ship

Helo—Helicopter

Hold—Cargo space in a ship

Holdback—Breakaway link that connects the nose tow to the catapult shuttle

Hook—Tailhook; a steel bar underneath the aircraft that snags the arresting hook

Hook Runner—The Green Shirt responsible for securing the aircraft to the catapult

Hornet—F/A-18 fighter-bomber

Hot Pump—Refueling an aircraft with the engines running

Intruder—A-6 attack aircraft

I/O—Indian Ocean

Island—The superstructure of an aircraft carrier

JBD—Jet Blast Deflector

Knot—Nautical mile per hour; about 1.15 miles per hour

KA-6D tanker, with folded wings.

LAMPS—Light Airborne Multi-purpose System; a shipborne helicopter and its associated electronic systems on board ship, used to prosecute submarines

Langley Stripe—A band of color on either side of the cockpits of some Navy fighters

LCAC—Landing Craft Air Cushion

LCM—Landing Craft, Mechanized; "Mike boat"

LCU—Landing Craft, Utility

Loose Deuce—A Navy tactical fighter formation

LPD—Amphibious transport (dock)

LSD—Landing ship (dock)

LSO—Landing Signal Officer

LVTP—Marines' workhorse landing craft

LVA—Experimental replacement for LTVP

MAD—Magnetic Anomaly Detector

Marshall—The holding pattern behind the carrier

Military—Military power; full engine thrust without using afterburner (also called "buster")

Modex—Three-digit code on the nose of carrier aircraft

Modloc—Modified local operating area; the perimeter of CVBG operations

Mouse—Two-way headsets worn by flight deck crewmen

Mule—Carrier aircraft tug; also called "Stubby"

NavAirSysCom—Naval Air Systems Command

NFO—Naval Flight Officer

Non-skid—Rubber-like coating compound used on the flight deck

Nose Tow—The part of the forward landing gear to which the catapult shuttle is attached

NTDS—Naval Tactical Data System; U.S. Navy voice and data-link network

Nugget—A rookie naval aviator

OOD—Officer of the Deck

Outlaw Shark—USN program for over-the-horizon targeting of cruise missiles

Overhead—The ceiling of a ship's cabin

P-School—A short course in flight ops for new carrier deck hands

P-12—Crash truck

PLAT Channel—Pilot's Landing Aid Television; a closed-circuit TV channel piped through the carrier that monitors the flight deck

Pack—A group of aircraft on deck

Pantry—The ship's food storeroom

Phalanx—Mk-15 CIWS (Close-in Weapons System); a six-barrel, antiaircraft Gatling gun

Phantom—F-4 fighter-bomber

PHM—Hydrofoil patrol boat

Phoenix—AIM-54 long-range air-to-air missile

Pickle—A switch held by the LSO to signal a wave-off to an aircraft attempting to land

Plane Guard—The helicopter or ship assigned to search and rescue during flight ops

Polaris—UGM-27; first generation USN submarine-launched strategic missile

Port—The left side of a ship

Poseidon—UGM-73; second generation USN submarine-launched strategic missile

Prairie Masker—USN ASW countermeasure

Pri-Fly—Primary Flight Control; the carrier's flight control center for launches and recoveries

Primary Air Controller—The Air Boss

Prowler—EA-6B electronic warfare aircraft

Purple Shirt—A carrier crewman assigned to refueling aircraft

Quartermaster—The ship's navigator

RI0—Radar Intercept Officer; the NFO "backseater" in an F-14 or F-4

Rack—Bunk

Ramp—The extreme aft end of the flight deck; also called the rounddown

Rank—Position in the military hierarchy, officer or enlisted man

Rate—The level of a rating

Rating—Occupations in the Navy

Ready Room—Squadron headquarters aboard the carrier

Red Shirt—Flight deck crewman assigned to ordnance handling

Retract Engine—Small motor that lifts the tailhook after landing

Roller—Navy slang for hot-dog

SAM—Surface-to-Air Missile
Scrubber—Vehicle that wipes seawater and fuel off the flight deck
Sea King—SH-3 helicopter
Second Fleet—USN East Coast fleet
Senso—Air crewman charged with ASW search
Seventh Fleet—USN Pacific fleet
Shooter—A warship equipped with surface-to-air missiles
Shuttle—That part of the catapult that attaches to the launching aircraft
Sidewinder—AIM-9 heat-seeking air-to-air missile
Sixth Fleet—USN Mediterranean fleet
SLEP—Service Life Extension Program; an extensive overhaul designed to prolong the use of Navy carriers
Slider—Navy slang for hamburger
Small Boy—Any small warship
Snipe—Engine-room worker
Sparrow—AIM-7 radar-guided air-to-air missile
SSM—Surface-to-Surface Missile
Stack—The ship's smokestack or funnel
Standard-ER—RIM-67 radar-guided, extended-range surface-to-air missile
Standard-MR—RIM-66 radar-guided, medium-range surface-to-air missile
Starboard—The right side of a ship
Stern—The aft end of a ship
Superstructure—The part of a ship above the hull, exclusive of armament
Surface Action Group—A task force organized around surface warships
TARPS—Tactical Air Reconnaissance Pod System; a recce pod slung underneath the F-14
Tacco—Air crewman charged with ASW attack

Tall Moose—Unusually high carrier landing
Tender—A ship that services a group of smaller vessels
Third Fleet—USN West Coast fleet
Three Wire—The third of four arresting cables, counting up from the stern
Tillie—Movable flight deck crane
Tomahawk—A family of USN long-range cruise missiles
Tomcat—F-14 fighter
Towed Array—A group of sonar sensors dragged behind the ship on a long cable
Trap—An arrested aircraft landing on a carrier
Trident—UGM-93; third generation USN submarine-launched strategic missile
URG—Underway Replenishment Group
USS—United States Ship
V/STOL—Vertical/Short Take-Off and Landing
VDS—Variable Depth Sonar
VLS—Vertical Launch System
Vampire—An incoming guided missile
Viking—S-3 ASW aircraft; the "Hoover"
Vulture's Row—The observation deck on the carrier's island
Wardroom—The officers' dining area
Weather Deck—The main deck of a ship
White Shirt—Plane inspector, also called "checker"
Wire—Arresting cable
XO—Executive Officer
Yankee Station—CVBG operating area in the South China Sea
Yellow Shirt—Aircraft movement director
Zone 5—Maximum thrust in afterburner

Chapter One

The Great Ocean

The Great Ocean rolls across more than two thirds of the earth. Six miles of water cover its deepest point; at its shallowest, it is the depth of a droplet vaporizing on a summer's beach. The Great Ocean freezes white at the ends of the earth and nearly steams in the middle. Seven seas, four oceans, countless gulfs, bays, rivers, lakes, and canals all flow into the Great Ocean. It can be blue and featureless, indistinguishable from the darkening sky. Or it can churn into an ever-changing range of white-peaked mountains, a chain of gray-green volcanoes quaking violently under the deck, spewing foam and mist. The Great Ocean is blue, gray, green, white and—if you hold a tiny drop of its 620 million cubic miles in your hand—utterly clear.

The Great Ocean is the highway of the world's commerce. Raw materials sail in, manufactured goods sail out. The actual numbers soon zoom into incomprehension. Sooner or later, coming or going, everything floats across the Great Ocean.

The almost daily advances in military technology have compressed time and space, but they have not lessened the sea's importance as a bulwark for some and an obstacle to others. All but

New Jersey during sea trials off California.

two of America's forty-odd allies lie overseas. American men and equipment must be shipped across the sea to fight, and, once there, they must be supported with more shipping. A contemporary American serviceman in the field will consume his weight in supplies—food, fuel and ammunition—every day. Only the sea can support such a heavy logistical burden. If, in the next war, the battle of the Great Ocean is lost, further battles cannot be won.

America, whether or not it ever realizes it, is a maritime power like virtually every other industrial nation. Western Europe must rely upon shipping to bring in the ten key minerals needed to fire the furnaces of industry. Japan is even more dependent. Neither area has any oil to speak of. The United States is better off only comparatively.

There is only one exception. The Soviet Union, with its vast, rich landmass and restricted economy, is the only major world power whose fortunes do not ride on the tides of the Great Ocean. The implications are complex and enormous.

With the semi-retirement of the Royal Navy, the USN has inherited the responsibility of keeping the Great Ocean open to the West. In peacetime, the American Navy strides across the one sea, showing the flag in countries beyond the compass of land bases and diplomacy. In war, it must keep the sea-lanes open and carry the fight to the enemy's strongholds. And in the war beyond the war, the USN maintains the black watch underneath the Great Ocean, always ready for the final battle.

It is an intricate and imposing mission, one not always understood by either the public or the other military services. Lately, however, the Navy has been caught in the searchlight of publicity. Perhaps more than any other service, the USN has benefited from the fiscal bonanza the Reagan administration has presented to the military. Some of the results are readily apparent—old battleships bristle with new weapons, aircraft carriers are building on the ways, and the superstructures of new warships tower in long dormant shipyards.

But the Navy's build-up is not without its critics. Some question the way the precious resources are being spent. It takes at least ten years for modern ships to make the voyage from the drawing boards to the Great Ocean. The American Navy of the next century is being launched today. Will a battleship built in the 1940s—however modernized—be able to cope with the threats of the year 2000? Even the new ships do not necessarily reflect new ideas. The next nuclear carriers are being built to a twenty-year-old design, though they are not scheduled to be retired until 2040. The latest cruisers boast a new anti-air defense system, but from the hull down, their design goes back nearly fifteen years.

It costs about $35 billion to buy a nuclear carrier battle group—the supercarrier, its aircraft, and its escorts—and run them for thirty years. Could that money be better spent? The tab for the Navy's newest aircraft, the F-18 Hornet, runs about $30 million. Is it worth it? The Navy wants a hundred nuclear attack submarines, at about $700 million a shot. Is it wise to invest that kind of money in a relatively untried weapons system?

The debate over defense costs is a common peacetime theme of the popular press. And certainly the Navy isn't the only service with a fondness for expensive hardware. When the bullets aren't flying, it's a tough call—all weapons are useless in peacetime and priceless in wartime.

But there is a more fundamental reason than dollars and cents to make sure the right weapons are built before the fighting. Long lead times and a vulnerable industrial base virtually ensures that the Navy would fight World War III with the weapons at hand. Is the Navy building the right ships, the right planes? Is the fleet they're building up to the monumental task of controlling the Great Ocean? Everyone has their own answers to those questions. We'll take a look at the modern American Navy—what it is, where it came from, and where it's going.

This would all be academic if it were not for the navy of the Soviet Union. The Soviet Navy has its own problems, but it is the American Navy's only real rival in the battle to control the Great Ocean. Neither Navy has experienced combat on the high seas since World War II, but unlike most Air Force and Army units, American Navy ships confront their Soviet counterparts every day. Each side gets a close-up look at its potential adversary, with the laws of the sea dictating that some of the confrontations fall just short of actual combat.

There is much to admire about the Soviet Navy, including their rapid progress and their willingness to innovate. There is also much to dislike. Contradictory reports of the worth of the Soviet Navy appear constantly in the press. We are concerned when the Soviets build ships similar to ours. We are concerned when they do not. We'll take a look at the Soviet Navy, too. But first, let's define what the navies are fighting for.

The Great Ocean covers 73 percent of the earth, but it is geography that determines which slivers of the sea the Navy is willing to fight and die for. The Great Ocean is vast, but, for the most part, militarily insignificant; oftentimes the sea assumes an importance inversely proportional to the amount of space it occupies between two land masses.

The places where the Great Ocean squeezes strategically are called "choke points". At these points great fleets can be bottled up, and small amounts of firepower can make a big difference. The current naval strategies of both superpowers are drafted around choke points, aimed either at forcing them open or keeping them corked. In the next war, terrible battles will be fought for tiny pieces of the Great Ocean. And the next war at sea will probably be decided there.

The Soviet Navy is particularly ill-placed in relation to choke points. At any given time, less than a quarter of its naval units are at sea. Due to maintenance and operational requirements, most of the Soviet fleet remains tied to the dock. Even the deployed units spend a great deal of time at anchor or under tow. In addition, the majority of Soviet naval units are based so near the Arctic Circle that the path to the open sea is blocked by ice much of the year. Geographically isolated, the Soviet fleets seeking to join up in wartime would have to brave the gamut of allied defenses waiting to mug them at the choke points.

The most important choke point runs from Greenland to Scotland. Called the Greenland-Iceland-U.K., or "GIUK Gap" (or for those who prefer a more mellifluous acronym, the British-Iceland-Greenland, or "BIG Gap"), it covers the area the Soviet Red Banner Northern Fleet would need to traverse to take up station in the Atlantic. Most of the fleet's muscle takes the form of submarines, so the western powers have weaved an underwater trap of sonar sensors, dormant minefields, attack submarine ambush areas, surface ship patrols, and antisubmarine aircraft pickets to bottle up the fleet before it reaches the sea lanes of the North Atlantic.

The Red Banner Baltic Fleet is also fenced in. The only way out is through the Kattegat, between Denmark and the southern tip of Sweden. The Baltic Fleet is not nearly as powerful as the Northern Fleet—the bulk of its units are small surface combatants and auxiliaries. Its most important function in peacetime is the operational testing of new ships. (The Soviet Union's largest shipbuilding and refit base is off the Baltic Sea at Leningrad.)

The fleet's wartime mission appears to be control of the Baltic Sea and its approaches—choke points swing both ways. The importance Moscow attaches to the mission is evidenced by the almost annual Soviet submarine sighting in Swedish territorial waters; details of the Swedish defenses must be particularly valuable to the Soviets to risk an international incident by getting caught scouting them out in peacetime. Sweden and the navies of NATO's northern tier will fight the bulk of the battle of the Baltic for the West.

The Soviet Pacific Fleet is more dispersed, but no less hemmed in. Its headquarters at Vladivostok and the new installations on Sakhalin Island are poorly placed. Japan's Kuril Islands block the gateway to the Bering Sea. Only the large submarine base at Petropavlovsk, on the eastern side of the Kamchatka Peninsula, is free from waters under Japanese control or observation, but it is also cut off from the rest of the Pacific Fleet's bases on the mainland.

Lately, the Soviet Union has virtually taken control of Cam Rahn Bay, the giant naval base built by the Americans in Vietnam. A number of reconnaissance planes and about thirty Soviet ships are rotated in and out, to provide an almost permanent Soviet presence in the South China Sea.

The Soviet Navy also has a large installation at Sovetskaya Gaven, southwest of Sakhalin Island. One can only guess that the Soviet command thought it was protecting the base from the prying eyes of an American spyplane when it shot down the Korean airliner over Soviet territory in 1983.

There is no hope at all for the Soviet Caspian Sea Flotilla to reach the Great Ocean. The body of water is completely enclosed by the Soviet Union on three sides, and, to the south, the northern coast of Iran. Like the Baltic Fleet, the Caspian Sea Flotilla serves a major role as a center for training recruits and testing naval weapon systems.

The Red Banner Black Sea Fleet is well situated for its primary mission. Headquartered at Sevastopol on the Crimean Peninsula, the fleet should have no trouble controlling the Black Sea—there is a disproportionately large number of ships in its inventory, as well as many aircraft, including Backfire bombers.

However, the reason the Black Sea Fleet is so well equipped is that it is also charged with maintaining the Soviet Mediterranean Squadron. The permanent presence of the Soviet Navy in the Med caused great consternation in the West when the Squadron first began to make its presence felt in the seventies.

However, in wartime, the Soviet Navy would have a tough time breaking out from the Black Sea into the Mediterranean, and an even tougher time should they try to venture out into the Atlantic. First, they would have to force their way through the Bosporus and Dardanelles straits, controlled

Right: An *Aegis* cruiser under construction in Pascagoula, Mississippi. The Navy plans to build three *Ticonderoga* class cruisers a year.

Below: Soviet helicopter carrier *Minsk* in the Med.

by Turkey, a NATO ally. Another bottleneck occurs as the fleet tries to go around the island of Crete through the straits of Karpathos and Kithira.

The Soviet position in the Mediterranean suffered considerably with the loss of Egypt as an ally. Its other friends in the region—Syria and Libya—are not so well-placed or as reliable as Egypt once was. Today, about two dozen ships and submarines are rotated to the Soviet Mediterranean Squadron from other fleets. The Soviet Navy generally confines itself to anchorages in the eastern Med, conducting antisubmarine patrols and keeping tabs on the American Sixth Fleet.

The West has its problems with choke points, as well. Most often mentioned is the Strait of Hormuz, separating the Persian Gulf from the Gulf of Oman and the Arabian Sea. The U.S. imports just a fraction of its oil from the Gulf states. If the pipes were shut off, America could probably get along without it. But our allies could not. Two thirds of the oil that runs the economies of Western Europe flows through the Strait of Hormuz. Almost all of Japan's oil comes from the region.

Iran and Iraq's grudge match has had little effect on the flow of oil from the Persian Gulf. Nearly all the well-publicized attacks on shipping have occurred at the northern end of the Gulf. The total number of ships attacked in the five years of the war barely exceeds the number of tankers that squeeze through the Strait of Hormuz in one day. At times, both Iran and Iraq have hinted at closing the strait, but such an action—if it could be done—would surely bring the hammer of Western military might down on the culprit and tip the balance to the other party. In a global war, however, closing the Strait of Hormuz and bottling up the Gulf's oil would be a major Soviet objective.

Oil on its way to Japan has to pass through another narrow choke point at the Strait of Malacca, between Malaysia and the island of Sumatra in the South China Sea. American naval units on peacetime patrol shoot the straits off Singapore on their way to the Indian Ocean, but there is a growing feeling that Japan should shoulder the responsibility of keeping the straits open in wartime.

Some of America's most vital choke points are right offshore in the Caribbean. The Yucatan Channel, off Mexico, and the Straits of Florida, off the Keys, control the entrance to the Gulf ports of Houston, New Orleans, and Tampa. Both are dominated by Cuba. Cuba also lies to one side of the Paso de los Viantos, off Haiti, the quickest route to the Panama Canal for ships leaving ports on the eastern seaboard. In wartime, of course, Cuba would be isolated and could probably not hold out for long. But the point is, even though the major American naval ports are well placed, the country cannot take its commercial ports for granted, at least in the opening stages of a war.

To keep up with the changing demands of power projection, the Navy has constructed a flexible, if bewildering, command hierarchy. The Navy's organization is tough to follow for two reasons. For one thing, naval units can be under two entirely different chains of command, one for day-to-day operations and another when deployed. And the grouping of units changes constantly.

There are four numbered fleets: The Second Fleet in the Atlantic Ocean, the Sixth Fleet in the Mediterranean Sea, the Third Fleet in the eastern Pacific Ocean, and the Seventh Fleet in the western Pacific and the Indian Ocean. The numbered fleets operate more or less the same types of ships and aircraft, but are quite different in character.

The carriers and their air wings are fairly evenly divided between the Atlantic and Pacific fleets. Although the Pacific fleets have more units, there are more combatants assigned to the Atlantic fleets. This reflects the greater burden of logistics in the Pacific and the greater Soviet presence in the Atlantic. Ironically, even though the newer types of ships and equipment usually make their debut in the Atlantic fleets—especially in the Sixth Fleet—the Pacific fleets enjoy greater prestige. This is because, in Europe, naval operations are

A Mexican patrol boat buzzes around the assault carrier *Tarawa* during exercises off Acapulco. In recent years the Navy has grown increasingly aware of growing threats in waters near the U.S. mainland.

generally subordinate to land operations, but the Pacific theater is essentially a Navy show. The Pacific was also the scene of the Navy's greatest triumphs during World War II. The situation is the reciprocal of the favored status that USAFE (United States Air Forces in Europe) has in the personnel files of Air Force fighter jocks.

The Second and Third fleets have the most ships assigned, but they are considered "non-deployed" fleets and are mainly concerned with training and maintenance. The Navy has gone to a philosophy of "Flex Ops"—instead of sailing circles in the ocean, ships are now usually deployed only for a specific task, usually an exercise. This keeps more units in reserve for crisis and helps the crews get more from each deployment. Ships assigned to these fleets *do* deploy on training cruises, of course, but the units that are rotated from these fleets to the forward fleets see most of the peacetime action.

The Second Fleet is headquartered at Norfolk, Virginia. It is the largest American naval base, and a prime target for a Pearl Harbor–style nuclear attack. Lately, naval planners have become worried about putting so many eggs in one basket, and now plan to base at least some of the carriers normally assigned to Norfolk—and to the naval base at San Diego, nearly as large—to selected ports along both coasts.

Most of the ships assigned to the forward fleets are rotated from the continental fleets for about six months. But the amount of time ships are assigned to the Sixth and Seventh fleets can vary greatly, depending on contingencies and the length of the cruise.

The commander of the Sixth Fleet runs the show from the headquarters in Gaeta, north of

Naples, or aboard his flagship, *Coronado,* a converted landing ship. Ships of the Sixth Fleet make port calls all around the Med. There are a couple of important logistics bases, most of them in the western Med. Naval Air Station Sigonella, Sicily, is a familiar roost for antisubmarine and electronic warfare aircraft. In 1978, Spain asked the United States to cease basing strategic missile submarines at Rota, but the port near Gibraltar is still an important supply point for the Sixth Fleet. The tender that supports the fleet's four or five nuclear-powered attack submarines is docked at La Maddalena, on the island of Sardinia. (The base is ringed by strong defenses manned by Italian troops, but that's as much to keep the sailors in as terrorists out; there is a Club Med on the other side.)

In the eastern Med, the realliance of Egypt to the West has given the Sixth Fleet much needed bases for naval operations near the Middle East. The fleet maintains a strong presence in both Greece and Turkey, although that's a volatile situation politically—both countries are nominal NATO allies, but they hate each other. The USN has grown closer to Israel as the Soviet presence in

Carrier *America* (CV-66), in the Med.

the eastern Med has increased. The Israeli port of Haifa was particularly busy during the recent crisis in Lebanon.

The Sixth Fleet used to have two carriers regularly assigned. But since the Iranian hostage crisis and the growing instability in the Persian Gulf, the Sixth Fleet is usually up to strength only during times of trouble, or when another carrier transits the Med on its way to the Indian Ocean. This changes as events warrant, however. The Navy managed to put three carriers off Beirut for a brief period in 1984.

The need for a permanent American naval presence in the Indian Ocean has also stretched the resources of the Navy's Pacific fleets. The Third Fleet provides the bulk of the forward-based Seventh Fleet, as well as support for Task Force 70, the Navy's Indian Ocean (I/O) detachment. The Indian Ocean, and especially the Persian Gulf, has drawn a lot of attention from the Pentagon lately, due to the mismatch of American strategic interests and American military muscle in the region.

The United States has worked hard to get bases in the area. They've had no luck in the Persian Gulf, where the sultan of Oman has turned down a request to base the headquarters of the new Central Command. He's worried that a permanent American presence would stir up Islamic fever among the population. The U.S. is hoping to establish a base on the island of Masirah, where American servicemen would be less visible, but still in position to move quickly in a crisis. Until then, the U.S. headquarters in the region operates out of a ship at sea, cutting circles in the water.

The Navy is also looking for friends in Africa. The U.S. has secured base rights in Kenya, Somalia, and Djibouti. Perhaps "secured" isn't the right word. Nothing is permanent in that part of the world, except, perhaps, hunger and revolution. The Navy is hedging its bets and holding onto Diego Garcia.

The little horseshoe-shaped spit of land at the end of the Indian Ocean doesn't look like one of

The new rocket cruiser *Slava,* one of many new warship types entering Soviet naval service.

the most important military bases in the world. Indeed, until the mid-seventies most people could be excused for thinking Diego Garcia was just a figment of the English imagination. The United States leased the base from the British after realizing that America's lack of bases anywhere near the scene of potential conflict in the region would make military intervention almost impossible.

This was in the days of the old Rapid Deployment Force (RDF), a unit that existed mainly on paper and was neither rapid nor deployable, and not much of a force (although the name was certainly less contentious than its original designation, the Unilateral Intervention Force). All of the units assigned to the RDF were actually based somewhere else, and most had other commitments, usually to the defense of NATO. Until the beginning of the annual Bright Star exercises, only the Navy had ever *seen* the Indian Ocean, and it's still the only service that maintains a permanent presence there.

Diego Garcia is five days steaming from the Persian Gulf, but it's brought logistical support a lot closer to the ships on Gonzo Station in the Arabian Sea. If the island is hard for Navy ships to reach, it's also out of the range of most adver-

saries. P-3 recon and antisubmarine aircraft stage out of "Dodge City," Navy slang for Diego Garcia, on their seventeen-hour patrols. The new landing strip can also accommodate Air Force B-52s. And in the newly dredged harbor there is enough room for ships packed with all the equipment needed by a Marine amphibious brigade.

The western Pacific is familiar territory to old Navy hands. In particular, the eastern coast of Asia is of vital interest to the Seventh Fleet. Although the Air Force has a few bases in South Korea and Japan, the Navy is the real American power in that part of the world.

The Pacific is huge. Even though the Navy is only concerned with tiny parts of it, the great expanse of the Pacific Ocean still plays a major part in Seventh Fleet operations. Most of its ships are logistic runners. They are on the move all the time, keeping the task forces thousands of miles from the nearest base supplied. A large part of each deployment is spent just getting to and from station.

To cut down on transit time, the Navy has stationed a carrier forward in Japan, at Yokosuka (pronounced "yoh-KOOS-kah"). Currently, *Midway* is so deployed, with its air wing stationed at nearby Atsugi. A number of ships operate from Subic Bay, an important American naval base in the Philippines.

Growing global commitments and block obsolescence of a number of ships built just after World War II has caused the Navy to clamor for more ships and more money. The Navy had more than a thousand ships in 1970. Ten years later, it was down to less than half that number. Significantly, the USN had lost more than half its aircraft carriers, as a number of World War II–era carriers reached the end of their service lives. But the Navy's commitments—and the size of the Soviet Navy—increased during the same time period, necessitating a major rebuilding program.

You hear a lot about the 600-ship Navy these days. Navy Secretary John Lehman set this number as one of his goals when he took office. Although it sounds like a nice round number conjured up to justify more shipbuilding, the number is actually the result of thousands of hours of computer time. The study took into account the Pentagon's impressions of the next war, the Navy's missions, and the Soviet threat. The needs and projected losses were fed in one end, and the number 600 came out the other.

It is important to keep in mind exactly what ships are included in the "600-ship Navy." After all, the Navy has more than that now. The 600-ship goal, however, doesn't include many types of auxiliaries (although it does include fleet oilers and ammunition ships that will go in harm's way to replenish the combatants at sea). Using the "battle forces" criteria, the Navy currently has just over 530 ships in commission.

The 600-ship Navy concept shouldn't be taken too literally. What the Navy really wants is enough ships-of-the-line to make up eight carrier battle groups (with two carriers in every group but one), four surface action groups centered around battleships, and enough escorts to protect one-and-a-half Marine amphibious forces, seven convoys, and ten underway replenishment groups. The figures actually add up to considerably more than 600 ships. But who's counting?

The Soviets, maybe. They've got three times as many hulls as the USN, but the numbers are skewed by a collection of old diesel attack submarines and the kind of small surface combatant ships the U.S. Navy doesn't want to build. The USN doesn't seem to know what to do with their *Oliver Hazard Perry* class frigate, the low end of Adm. Elmo Zumwalt's "high-low mix." The Navy considers it too slow and too lightly armed to take part in carrier battle group operations. But the *Perry* is a heavyweight compared with most warships in the Soviet Navy.

On the other hand, the Soviet Union has a very small number of very large ships, and the number is growing as the Russian Navy wades out from its coasts into deeper water. As its missions change, the design of its ships changes as well. For years, the Soviet Navy was built for a one-shot war. Its mission was to deny the West control of the sea by ambushing its ships with quick, devastating attacks. Soviet maritime design reflected this by building ships with few, if any, main armament reloads, little damage control capability, and spartan crew quarters.

Now, as the Soviets move from sea denial to sea control, their fleet is growing up. It's no coincidence Russian ships are starting to resemble their Western counterparts; the difference has always been mission-oriented, not national. Their new *Udaloy* class destroyers are strikingly similar to the American *Spruance,* for example. It's not a question of imitation. The Soviets have always displayed a willingness to go their own way on ship design. It's just that both ships share the same mission—open ocean antisubmarine warfare (ASW).

The Russians may have bitten off more than they could chew in their hurry to join the big leagues of blue water ops. Despite the construc-

The F/A-18 Hornet is slated to replace both the F-4 and the A-7 on carrier flight decks.

tion of new, dedicated underway replenishment ships and an intense study of how the experts in the U.S. Navy do it, the Soviets may find that keeping their big new ships sailing will be a big headache. And if shooing submarines away from the carrier battle group on the high seas is tough for the USN, it's bound to be a nightmare for the Soviets, with their less sophisticated ASW systems.

But the biggest problem the Russians face is lack of air power on the Great Ocean. They're trying to remedy that by building a new carrier, which we'll take a look at later. Now let's look at the principal warships in the American fleet.

First, a word about nomenclature. Navy ships are all assigned a name and a hull number. Ships used to be christened according to set guidelines. For example, all battleships were named after states. This procedure is no longer followed with any regularity. After the U.S. stopped making battleships, cruisers were named for states. Carriers used to be named after ships that were named after famous Revolutionary War battles. Now cruisers are named after carriers that were named after ships that were named after Revolu-

tionary War battles. And ballistic missile submarines are named after states. You get the idea. If it sounds confusing, it's because it is.

Hull numbers are straightforward only by comparison. The designation consists of a type —cruiser, destroyer, whatever—and a series number. The designation contains the first letter of the type as its first letter, plus other letters denoting special characteristics and abilities. CGN 38, for example, is the thirty-eighth modern cruiser (C), which happens to be able to launch guided missiles (G) and is nuclear powered (N).

CGN 38 is the U.S.S. *Virginia,* usually called simply the Virginia or just *Virginia* (the Navy has a thing against articles). *Virginia* is the lead ship of the *Virginia* class. That is, it's the first of that design built. The other three ships built to that design are said to be *Virginia* class cruisers (or CGN 38 class cruisers).

The roles of modern warships have changed since World War II, and the distinctions between types of warships have been blurred. For example, most American cruisers seem small compared to their World War II counterparts, but they are huge for frigates, which is how most of them started life.

The ships didn't grow, but their role did. With the swipe of a pen on June 30, 1975, the USN lost a bunch of DGLN's (guided missile light destroyers or destroyer leaders) and gained the same number of cruisers. The move was taken to more accurately reflect the capability of the ships, especially compared to the relatively lightly-armed warships the Russians were calling cruisers. A similar threat inflation took place when, at the same time, some frigates were promoted to destroyers. Well, it's one way to improve your order of battle.

The American Navy seems, at first, to contain almost as many classes as ships. But closer examination shows that most of the later classes are merely improvements on a previous design.

For example, even the latest American carriers can trace their design back directly to *Forrestal*, the first of the supercarriers (whose design, in turn, borrowed heavily from the *United States*, an ambitious post-war carrier canceled one day after construction began). There are four carriers in the *Forrestal* class, the others being *Saratoga, Ranger,* and *Independence*. All were built before 1960. Their nominal service lives run out at the end of this decade, but all are undergoing extensive rebuilding that will allow them to sail in the next century.

The earlier *Midway* class carriers have long since reached the end of their projected time in service, but soldier on regardless. Laid down on battleship hulls during World War II, they were the first American warships too big to slip through the Panama Canal. Six were ordered, but only three were built. *Franklin D. Roosevelt* was retired after being grounded, leaving only *Midway* and *Coral Sea*.

Both *Midway* and *Coral Sea* have been exten-sively modernized, but neither can operate the big F-14 Tomcat fighters or S-3 Viking ASW aircraft. With a smaller flight deck and only three arresting cables and two catapults, they just don't have the room to operate the large aircraft safely. Both will receive the new F/A-18 Hornet to replace the F-4 in the fighter role. *Midway* is in better shape; based forward in Japan, it spends more than two thirds of its time at sea. *Coral Sea*—the "ageless warrior"— has already undergone refit to operate Hornets.

The four ships of the *Kitty Hawk* class are almost identical to the *Forrestals,* although somewhat larger. The port lift was repositioned aft from the end of the flight deck, where it was useless much of the time. In addition, the island was also positioned farther aft, with two of the three starboard elevators forward. The other *Kitty Hawks* are *Constellation, America,* and *John F. Kennedy* (although the Navy officially considers *JFK* a separate class).

The design was retained for the *Nimitz* class carriers, although, since the ships are nuclear powered, there is more internal storage space for fuel and ammunition. There are four *Nimitz* carriers—*Nimitz, Dwight D. Eisenhower, Carl Vinson,* and *Theodore Roosevelt*—with two more, *Abraham Lincoln* and *George Washington* building. They are the largest warships in the world.

The Navy pioneered the concept of the nuclear-powered aircraft carrier with the *Enterprise*. Six were planned, but, as is so often the case, the ship proved too expensive and only one was built. Originally fitted with a distinctive pineapple-shaped island with built-in "billboard" radar aerials, the design proved a maintenance nightmare. *Enterprise* was rebuilt with a more conventional island during her last major refit.

The cruiser *Long Beach* was given a similar facelift during her recent modernization. The careers of *Long Beach* and *Enterprise* have been intertwined from their conception. Built to test the

Nuclear-powered attack submarine *La Jolla* passes the nuclear-powered guided missile cruiser *Long Beach* in San Diego harbor.

concept of nuclear power at sea, the two ships, along with the nuclear-powered *Bainbridge,* took off on a round-the-world cruise in 1964, without once stopping to refuel.

Long Beach has a history of being armed with phantom weapons systems. The ship was originally designed to carry Regulus cruise missiles. When that program was canceled, the intention was to arm *Long Beach* with Polaris ballistic missiles. That plan was scrapped also, and the cruiser entered service without any antisurface armament whatsoever. It was the first warship ever built armed only with missiles, although two 5″ guns were later added amidships. In the same refit in which her "billboard" radars were replaced, *Long Beach* received two Phalanx antiaircraft guns and two quad launchers for the Harpoon cruise missile.

Although *Long Beach* was basically a one-off design, the rest of the Navy's cruisers can trace their design back to *Leahy.* The two ships were built almost simultaneously in the early sixties, a time when the Navy was convinced that the gun was an anachronism at sea. The ships were built with two 3″ gun mounts, poorly placed amidships. (The guns are now being removed to make way for Harpoon launchers). The nine *Leahy*s were built for antiair carrier escort, and are "double-ended" —that is, they have guided missile launchers fore and aft. At congressional insistence, one of the *Leahy*s was nuclear powered. *Bainbridge* is distinguished by her lack of "macks"—the combined mast and stack arrangement introduced in *Leahy.*

The subsequent nine-ship *Belknap* class is very similar in design. Its members differ from the slightly smaller *Leahy*s in that they have full helicopter support facilities (the *Leahy* class cruisers have a helicopter pad, but no hangar) and a 5″ gun in place of the aft missile launcher.

Once again, Congress directed that one of the ships be driven by nuclear power: *Truxtun* is *Belknap*'s nuclear-powered half sister. Slightly larger, *Truxtun* also has the missile and gun mounts reversed.

With the building of the *Nimitz* class nuclear-powered aircraft carriers, the Navy set about to construct a new class of nuclear-powered cruisers to protect them. Once again, the basic *Leahy* design was used, with major modifications. *California* and *South Carolina* are much larger, with two 5″ guns, as well as missile launchers fore and aft.

The four cruisers of the *Virginia* class are similar in design, with *California*'s ASROC mount replaced by multi-purpose missile launchers. The *Virginia*s also carry a helicopter elevator and hangar aft, although the chopper is not usually embarked when the cruiser is on its primary mission of carrier escort.

Critics have attacked the Navy for building cruisers whose only job is to defend aircraft carriers from air and submarine attacks. They say the ships cannot operate independently, as cruisers have traditionally done, and, in fact, are helpless outside the protection of a task force.

But the criticism fails to take in several points. The first is, *no* ship can operate independently today. Every surface warship depends upon the layered defense of the task force to survive. And, though it's true that the cruisers, as originally built, sacrificed antisurface weapons in favor of AA and ASW systems, the ships are being refit with Harpoon, and, in some cases, Tomahawk cruise missiles for anti-ship punch. They're also being back-fitted with Phalanx antiaircraft guns for close-in protection, another much-needed capacity. With the addition of the new systems, the Navy's cruisers have matured into well-balanced fighting ships, easily the equal of any at sea today.

The Navy has closed the book on the *Leahy*-style cruisers. The newest cruisers sliding down the

---

Standard ER (extended range) surface-to-air-missile fired from the cruiser *Wainwright* off San Juan, Puerto Rico. *General Dynamics photo.*

Spruance class destroyer *Elliot* in mirror-like seas.

ways are the *Ticonderoga* class. Built around the *Aegis* integrated combat system, the *Ticonderoga* cruisers are built primarily to defend the carrier battle group against cruise missile attacks. But the *Ticonderoga*s also have a potent antisubmarine and antisurface capability. We'll discuss the *Tico* and its *Aegis* weapons system in detail later in this book.

The *Ticonderoga* is built on the hull of the *Spruance* class destroyer, the Navy's premier sub-hunter. *Spruance* is *not* a well balanced ship. Although they carry the Harpoon anti-ship missile, the thirty-one *Spruance*s must depend on short-ranged missiles for air defense (though two Phalanx mounts are being added during refit). The Navy has announced plans to refit the *Spruance*s with Tomahawk cruise missiles. Some will be backfit with eight Tomahawks in a cannister launcher, but most will get a vertical launching system capable of holding a mix of sixty-one missiles. But the ships are very good at what they do. Big and roomy, they are excellent helicopter platforms, even in rough weather. They are also fast enough to keep up with the carrier battle group, yet quiet enough to hear subs without making too much noise themselves.

Some of the *Spruance*'s shortcomings were

U.S. Navy's newest guided missile cruiser, *Arkansas* (CGN-41), underway.

Oliver Hazard Perry (FFG-7), lead ship of the Navy's newest and largest class of frigates, undergoes a shock test.

remedied in the *Kidd* class destroyers. The ships fairly bristle with weapons, including the long-range Standard surface-to-air missile system. In fact, all the *Spruance*s were supposed to have been built to this design, but as the program grew more costly, the antiair role was de-emphasized. The four *Kidd*s were originally built for the Shah of Iran, but were snapped up cheap by a grateful Navy when the Shah fell from power. The *Kidd*s are thus known, unofficially, as the "Ayatollah" class destroyers.

The rest of the Navy's destroyers are "shooters" —antiaircraft escorts for the carrier battle groups. The ten *Coontz* class and twenty-three *Charles F.*

Adams class guided-missile destroyers were built in the early sixties, and their old-fashioned separate masts and funnels make them look even older. But these are very capable ships, with firepower equal to many Navy cruisers.

The Navy is building a new class of destroyers to replace these ships. The *Arleigh Burke* will be equipped with a version of the *Aegis* combat system now fitted to the *Ticonderoga* cruisers. *Burke* seems to have qualities of "Stealth" embedded in her design: with sleek lines and contoured stacks, the ship appears to have been built with a low radar signature in mind from the beginning. As with later ships in the *Ticonderoga* class, *Burke* will do away with conventional missile launchers in favor of a vertical launching system. The VLS will allow the ship to put more missiles in the air, as well as allowing the skipper more flexibility in the types of missiles launched. But the casual observer will see yet more empty deck space, and wonder why Navy ships are progressively disarming themselves.

The Navy's frigate programs have always been controversial. The problem, it seems, is that these ships, built for convoy escort, are at a loss during peacetime when there are no convoys to protect. The Navy keeps trying to force the frigates into carrier battle group escort duty, but the little ships, built to do everything reasonably well, can't do anything well enough to fit into any of the specialized roles needed in a battle group.

The *Oliver Hazard Perry* frigates, in particular, have gotten a bad rap. The purpose of the program was to put a large number of hulls in the water in a short period of time. This was accomplished; the *Perry* is the largest class of warships in the Navy's inventory. But it was built with cost-effectiveness in mind, and to Navy brass, this translates into "cheap." The *Perry*s have been called the "Chevettes of the Navy." It is ironic that the USN, which is constantly clamoring for more ships, is doing all it can to get rid of the *Perry*s. They've already transferred some to the

Naval Reserve, and there's talk of shuffling others off to the Coast Guard.

What's wrong with the *Perry*s? On paper, they are very formidable warships for their size. They carry Harpoon, ASROC, and Standard missiles, and a 3″ gun. But in order to save money, many critical systems, such as LAMPS helicopters and a Phalanx gun, were to be backfit later on. And they are susceptible to critical hits; all the missiles are fired from a single, one-armed launcher. If that goes, the ship is virtually defenseless. The same is true for the *Perry's* single screw, although a pair of retractable bow thrusters can be used to get the ship home in an emergency.

The ten *Garcia* class frigates are also powered by a single propeller, the only thing keeping them from being classified as destroyers. They are certainly as large and capable as many destroyers,

Knox class frigate *Pharris* participating in Unitas exercises off the coast of South America.

with two 5″ guns and full ASW helicopter facilities. The six *Brooke* class frigates are identical, with the exception of a Tartar missile launcher installed in place of the aft gun mount.

The forty-six *Knox* class frigates are good ASW ships, which is their primary function. They are almost helpless against air threats, with only a single, short-range missile launcher (once again, Phalanx will be backfit into these ships). The *Knox* frigates are distinguished by their circular mack, which looks like a castle turret rising amidship.

But hardware is only half the story. Ships need crews to sail and fight them. Let's take a look at the men who make up the American Navy.

Chapter Two

The Tick of a Ship

The Navy is run by one man. Not the chief of naval operations, or the secretary of the Navy, or even the president. The Captain runs the Navy, as he has since men started sailing on the Great Ocean. There are as many captains as there are ships, but—and this is important—only one captain on each ship.

He may not even wear the four stripes of a captain's rank. On Navy ships smaller than a cruiser, a commander, a lieutenant commander, or even a lieutenant may be in charge. But although the man in charge isn't always a captain, he *is* always the Captain.

Captains are individuals, certainly, with different leadership styles. But when command falls on a person's shoulders, something strange happens. Nice guys get a little meaner. Tough guys soften around the edges. The individual's personality becomes absorbed by the archetype.

No one knows exactly what makes a good captain, but everyone recognizes it. He is consistent in a changing world. He is calm when others are not. He is kind when the situation calls for it, stern when he has to be, fair only in the sense that nature is fair.

Yes indeed, he moves in mysterious ways. The captain never seems to *do* anything. Perched on his high chair in the highest part of the ship, he spends the day like one of the ancient gods. Individuals and incidents are brought to him for judgment. He dispenses justice with a nod of the head or a flick of the pen. He is always right, because he is the captain. How could he be wrong?

The captain has his military superiors, of course. Enlisted men say it hurts their eyes to look at admirals. More than any other service, Navy brass favor themselves with perks of office. Even within the spartan confines of a warship, ranking officers have their own staterooms, sometimes two—a sea cabin *and* an in-port cabin for entertaining.

The admiral eats alone, if he wants. Alcohol is forbidden on Navy warships—even such party animals as fighter pilots have to content themselves with weak fruit juice (called "bug juice") at sea. But no one's going to report the odd toast in the flag quarters. And while everyone else has to climb ladder after ladder, there is an elevator on most aircraft carriers reserved solely for the brass. The elevator, and the heights it rises to, are considered "Flag Country." Any mere, unauthorized mortal who dares approach is likely to get bounced out on his aft end by the marines of the admiral's private Praetorian Guard.

But even the bigwigs envy the ship's captain. Although there are many exceptions, the Navy

New Jersey's exec, the captain's right-hand man.

usually allows only one major at-sea command in each person's career. That tour is cherished, and while many enlisted men spend most of their time trying to figure out how to get off the ship, high-ranking naval officers spend the rest of their careers scheming to get back to sea.

But absolute power has its price. Let the captain screw up just once—even if it isn't remotely his fault—and he'll finish his career on shore somewhere counting widgets. The Navy giveth and the Navy taketh away.

If the captain seems to have one foot on Mount Olympus, the executive officer has both feet firmly on earth. The XO is to the CO as the agent is to the Hollywood star. The captain cannot be bothered with details and petty discipline. That's

the exec's job. The executive officer translates the captain's will into action. A good one will anticipate the captain's orders before they're given. Good execs are rewarded with a command of their own. Bad ones will not be execs for very long.

The captain and the exec run the ship through departments, some of which are broken down into divisions. These are the basic working groups of the Navy. The officers and men on board the Navy's ships often seem to be merely along for the ride, but each person on board has a definite job to do, much like the crew of an aircraft.

At the heart of a fighting ship is the Operations Department, headed by the ship's ops officer. On most warships, this department is broken down into several divisions. For example, the OC division handles communications (and, on an aircraft carrier, the control of air traffic). OA division is responsible for intelligence, while the OI division mans the combat information center.

The CIC (combat information center) is where the captain will fight the ship. On older warships, it's located behind the bridge, but on newer ships, the CIC is buried below for more protection. The Tactical Action Officer is the captain's representative in the CIC, just as the Officer of the Deck is his man on the bridge. The TAO stands his watch in the CIC, sometimes assisted by special deputies responsible for particular types of combat.

The OOD is the man in charge on the bridge. In most cases, he has the watch and the "conn," which means, in nautical terms, that he is in charge of the ship and its direction. The conn is an old Navy term for control of the ship (this explains the old submarine term "conning tower," which is now usually referred to as the submarine's sail). A slang term for the conn is the "bubble." On sailing ships the only instrument was a carpenter's level, and the pilot was obliged to keep the bubble in the middle (and the ship upright). The opposite of "having the bubble" is, of course, "losing the bubble"—losing control of the ship's movements. This could have disastrous consequences, both for the ship and for the careers of the men involved.

What sort of things can go wrong? To start with, there are the all-too-common navigational accidents. For the layman, it's hard to understand how ships can collide in the middle of the ocean —for sailors, it's hard to understand why it doesn't happen more often.

It's a matter of physics. It takes a lot to get a deep-draft ship moving, and, inertially speaking, even more to stop it. Turning the ship is easier, though not by much, but sometimes you don't have that option. The laws of the sea are very specific about rights of way, and often the only thing a crew can do is stay the course and hope the other ship lives up to its responsibility. The situation is made worse by the fact that communication with the oncoming ship is frequently impossible, either in English, or with code flashes or flags.

The other ship could be a supertanker with no one alert on the bridge. With such small crews these days, it's not uncommon for commercial vessels to cruise at night on "Iron Mike" —automatic pilot. Or the oncoming ship could be a drug-runner or smuggler. Navy men see some strange sights on the Great Ocean. But unless they are specifically ordered to interdict—as part of a blockade, for example—the USN gives a wide berth to even the most suspicious looking craft. It's none of their business.

Probably the biggest menace to navigation, for the USN, is the Soviet Navy. The superpowers rub elbows every day on the high seas, and they used to scrape a lot of paint. But things have improved since the "Incidents at Sea" talks in the seventies. Actually, it's the intelligence trawlers that really get to American sailors. The Soviet intelligence ships know the laws of the sea and use the letter of the law, if not the spirit, to their advantage. The nimble AGI craft can maneuver into the path of an oncoming carrier and then legally force the flattop to change course. Many a carrier skipper has wanted to ram the little trawlers, and there have been several close calls. Some USN officers

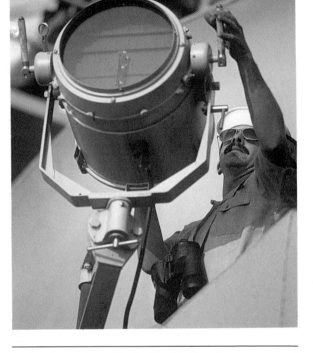

A signalman aboard the battleship *New Jersey* communicates with another ship during an EMCON environment.

think the rest of the Soviet Navy is ashamed of the tricks practiced by the spook fleet, but even American sailors offer grudging respect for the seamanship of the trawler skippers.

In the event of trouble, the ship's log acquires life-and-death importance. Actually, there are several logs. There's the main one, kept on the navigation bridge. There's also a log in the combat information center, another in the engine room, and so on. Any changes have to be initialed. The logs are archived, and any time there's an incident they are collected and locked up for safekeeping till they are handed over to the board of inquiry. On at least one ship a brush and a can of shellac were kept handy so important pages could be shel-

The bridge crew mans the watch.

lacked to prevent tampering.

To help him con the ship, the officer of the deck has a number of helpers. Although the names may change, the duties are the same throughout most navies. The most important enlisted man on the bridge is the Boatswain's Mate of the Watch. A petty officer, the BMOW makes sure all watch stations are manned and ready. He's the "strawboss" on the bridge, and, as one of the more experienced men on the navigation watch, oversees the work of the other enlisted watch standers.

The man with his hand on the wheel is the helmsman, or steersman. He steers the course given him by the OOD, using a compass repeater —the ship's main gyrocompass is usually located well below. The master compass drives most of the other compasses on board, to make sure all the departments are, literally, heading in the same direction. Navy ships still use a big wheel to direct the angle of rudder deflection, but instead of being spoked like a riverboat wheel, the inside of the wooden helm is filled in with a solid piece of polished brass.

The lee helmsman is a second steersman, in charge of transmitting speed and rpm changes ordered by the OOD to the engine room. In older ships, this is done by means of the engine order telegraph, another antique-looking brass affair that uses pulleys connected to bells to communicate speed and rpm changes to the sailor standing watch in the engine room. The engine room watch adjusts the speed and notifies the bridge that it has complied with the order by setting the answering pointer on *its* engine order telegraph to the same sector, from flank speed (fastest) to full speed astern (for a crash stop). The ship can be steered from aft steering in an emergency. In newer ships, speed can be controlled directly from the bridge, by means of a mechanism that increases or decreases propeller shaft revolutions per minute.

The quartermaster makes sure the ship is on the course set by the navigator. Along with the OOD, the quartermaster sets the ship's course and keeps the log on the navigation bridge. He works in the charthouse, which is usually just a section at the rear of the bridge with a large flat table cluttered with charts and drafting instruments. At night, the charthouse is curtained off to keep the light from ruining the night vision of the rest of the bridge watch.

On larger warships there is also a Plan Position Indicator. This is a large sheet of glass etched with the ship's position at the center of a circle showing the relative bearings of the other ships in the task force. The positions are updated by a sailor, as directed by the quartermaster or the OOD.

Ships are guided by a variety of navigational aids. Loran (long-range navigation) depends on a chain of radio transmitters set up by the Coast Guard. Omega is an expansion of the Loran system worldwide. Shoran is a variation of the Air Force's beacon bombing system, and uses transmitters placed on shore for triangulation of position. Radar and the sonar signals of a fathometer are also used to determine the ship's position.

These systems are accurate, but might not be available in wartime. Broadcasting stations can be destroyed and radar transmissions can be jammed or used to betray the ship's position to the enemy. The Navy prefers to use self-contained navigation-

Above: A snipe among the boilers. In an emergency the ship can be steered from the engine room.

al systems that are likely to survive after the shooting starts.

Satellite navigation data is highly accurate and almost impossible to jam. Older systems had their drawbacks. Often ships had to wait more than two hours for a satellite pass, especially near the equator. But when the new NAVSTAR global positioning satellites are fully deployed, instant directions from the heavens will become a reality for most warships.

But ships that will play a role in the black

Right: Launch control console aboard the submarine *Ohio* on patrol under the Atlantic.

"Holystoning" *New Jersey*'s teak deck. So far the Navy has had no trouble finding crews for the battlewagons.

theater of nuclear war cannot depend upon satellites, which are prime targets in an all-out conflict. Ballistic missile submarines and aircraft carriers have SINS, an inadvertently appropriate acronym that stands for Ship's Internal Navigation System. This is similar to an aircraft's inertial guidance system. All the navigator needs to know is the longitude and latitude of the port as the ship gets underway. The system's gyros and accelerometers keep up with every movement of the ship from then on. In ballistic missile subs, the missiles' guidance systems are patched into SINS, and that position is referenced so the birds can hit their targets from any point under the ocean.

To keep in practice—and to check the accuracy of the electronic guidance systems which no one in the Navy seems to trust fully, anyway—most navigators still use the ancient ways of finding one's way across the Great Ocean. Navy navigators are still adept at dead reckoning and taking star sightings with a sextant. And all the high-tech gear in the world won't help in getting a huge whale of a ship safely into harbor. Entering and leaving port is one of the trickiest evolutions in a ship's cruise, and one in which accidents are common.

Although today's sailors don't have to contend with mainsails and flying jibs, there is still a lot of seamanship involved in the contemporary Navy. It is, if anything, harder to operate modern ships because, in addition to routine nautical jobs like weighing the anchor and securing the deck, there are technical tasks that would baffle even World War II seamen.

The Deck Department is in charge of most duties one associates with the operation of a ship at sea. The "deck apes" haul the lines, swab the deck, man the boats, stow the cargo, and provide the muscle for the dozens of dirty little jobs that have to be done. The Deck Department is where most seamen start their careers. It gives them incentive to strike for a less strenuous rating.

The Engineering Department keeps the ship moving. In larger ships, it's broken down into several divisions—B division for boilers, M division for main engines, and so forth. The life of a "snipe" is not too much fun, either. In the hot climates—that is, where most of the Navy's ships tend to linger for months on end—temperatures down below can reach 120 degrees. And stay there. For months on end.

It's no wonder the snipes often envy the Weapons Department personnel. Oh, some of them, such as the poor saps doomed to handle ordnance, sweat as much as anyone on board. But the "twidgets" are another story.

Twidgets are fire control technicians who cruise across the ocean high and dry in the air-conditioned comfort of the F-division spaces. The twidget is a nautical version of the civilian "computer nerd." A twidget is seldom without his "tweaker"—a small, clip-on screwdriver used to make minor adjustments to equipment. To a real twidget, it's a badge of office. The rest of the ship's company have other names for it.

The weapons spaces are not cooled for the technician's benefit. Ships built before the widespread use of solid-state electronics carry a giant vacuum tube called a magnetron. When it works, the magnetron powers the ship's search radars. But the magnetron is high-strung and delicate, much like the twidgets who handle it. At high temperatures, the magnetron is prone to melt down, taking the ship's eyes and ears down with it. After a great many awkward—and expensive—magnetron blow-outs, even the U.S. Navy got the message. Now those spaces are air-conditioned, a rare luxury at sea. The twidgets say it's a lucky coincidence. The deck apes sniff a plot.

There is at least one other air-conditioned space on most ships. The crypto room is usually located between the bridge and the CIC. Access is restricted to a few officers and enlisted men. Most crewmen consider the Navy's fascination with codes and ciphers a real pain. Except in warmer climates. There, the air-conditioned crypto room is usually staffed around the clock.

In nuclear-powered ships, there is another department responsible for keeping the reactors running smoothly and safely. The Navy has not been very forthcoming concerning press accounts of alleged nuclear reactor incidents at sea. Such episodes appear to have been confined to nuclear-powered submarines and probably took place long ago. At any rate, the Navy is certainly much more careful with their nuclear power plants than the Soviets. Tales of hairless submariners and jokes about crewmen who glow in the dark are commonplace in the Soviet services. Admiral Hyman Rickover, the father of the American nuclear navy, says he received more radiation during a short tour of a Russian submarine than he did in all his years around the U.S. Navy's nuclear power plants. In contrast, Rickover says no American sailor has exceeded the maximum allowable dosage since 1967.

USN ships are generally much safer than Russian vessels. It's a combination of their design and the people who run them.

The Soviet Union does not have a great seafaring tradition. Generally, the Soviet sailor is a conscripted peasant who has never seen the ocean before being drafted. Their navy is especially weak in the petty officer corps, a rank whose experience, it is widely felt, is what really keeps the American Navy afloat. For the coronation of Queen Elizabeth II in 1953, the Soviet Union dispatched the cruiser *Sverdlov* to Great Britain. The English were very impressed by the seamanship displayed by the crew, as well they should have been; it was

later discovered that every man on board was an officer, hand-picked for the occasion.

Cramped as they are, American ships are luxury liners compared to Soviet vessels. Russian warships look more formidable, but it is an illusion created by putting all the weapons above deck on a very small hull. Although the ships are comparatively smaller, they are less automated than American ships, so more crewmen have to be crammed into smaller spaces. Doubling up is common practice; it is a rare sailor who has his own bunk aboard a Soviet ship. Space below is so crowded and stifling it is not uncommon to see Russian seamen sacked out on deck in the warmer latitudes.

Soviet ships are also lacking in compartmentalization and damage control. The two factors could spell disaster in battle. The effects are felt even in peacetime: In 1974 the destroyer *Otvazhny* suffered an explosion, burned to the waterline, and sank in the Black Sea with almost all of its three hundred men on board, while the captain waited for permission to flood the hold.

The USN has had its peacetime accidents, as well. For example, nearly *every* American aircraft carrier has figured in at least one major accident:

Nimitz suffered a major tragedy at sea in 1981, when an aircraft missed a night landing and plowed into a pack of parked aircraft—fourteen crewmen were killed and nearly fifty injured.

Forrestal went through a series of fires, including a major conflagration, while on station off North Vietnam (and was instantly dubbed the "Forest Fire" by Navy wags).

Constellation had a fire while under construction in the New York Naval Shipyard in 1960. (*Connie* was built at the same time as *Enterprise*, the Navy's first nuclear-powered carrier; since then, the ship has been disparagingly called the *Constellation Prize.*)

Fantail of a Soviet destroyer. Crew quarters aboard Soviet ships are much more cramped than those of American counterparts.

John F. Kennedy collided with the cruiser *Belknap* off Sicily in 1975. *Big John* escaped pretty much unharmed, but *Belknap* underwent reconstruction so extensive that it's now considered a separate class.

Ranger had an engine room fire off Central America not too long ago.

Coral Sea suffered damage in a collision with an Ecuadorian tanker in the Caribbean. Ironically, the *Coral Maru* had just emerged from an extensive refit in Norfolk.

Kitty Hawk had to undergo repairs after a Soviet submarine tried to surface with the *Hawk's* 80,000 tons on her back.

Enterprise had a fire in 1969 that set off nine major caliber bombs on the flight deck.

Franklin D. Roosevelt—the third *Midway* class carrier—was grounded so badly she was soon retired (although the Navy, which was lobbying for nuclear-powered flattops at the time, probably gave *Roosevelt's* skipper a medal for giving them a reason to replace it).

The Navy likes to point to these accidents as evidence that the carriers are tough enough to take it. Sure, they'll take hits, say Navy brass, but the

Opposite: The "twidgets" of the ship's weapons department let one fly. *General Dynamics photo.*

armored flight deck, side armor protection, good compartmentalization, and efficient damage control measures will enable the supercarriers to keep on fighting.

On the other hand, aircraft carriers, with their volatile fuel lines and ordnance exposed on deck while air operations are conducted, are particularly susceptible to catastrophic peacetime accidents. Other types of surface warships have much better safety records. But every ship practices damage control measures constantly. It's one of the things that sets the USN apart from the Soviet Navy, whose sailors have neither adequate training nor adequate equipment. It could make a big difference when the missiles start flying.

The Damage Control Assistant is attached to the engineering department. He supervises the training of the crew in damage control measures and checks the ship's emergency preparations. In battle, he mans Damage Control Central, keeping track of casualties, damage to the ship, and corrective measures taken. The information is provided by at least eight repair parties, each responsible for different sections of the ship.

Timing is critical in the dangerous business of carrier ops: crewmen crowd around an F-14 about to be launched; as soon as that plane is airborne, they prepare immediately for the next launch. *Photos by Michael Skinner.*

All seamen are trained in damage control. A course in firefighting is given to every recruit in basic training. Most are also introduced to at least the basics of first aid. In the battle drill, every crewman on board has a station, and a part in damage control operations.

The ships are built to minimize battle damage, and keep fire and flooding from spreading. Compartmentalization is vital to counter damage and to keeping the ship afloat. Navy ships are divided into watertight and airtight compartments by bulkheads and decks. Connected by secure hatches, the compartments can be sealed off to prevent flames or toxic gas from spreading. They can also be flooded to put out fires and provide ballast to keep a damaged ship from tilting over.

Compartments of ships built after 1949 are given a four-part alphanumeric code according to deck, frame, side, and type of space. This

"address" is similar to the way rooms in the Pentagon are designated, and is just as confusing to anyone who has never served in the military. On destroyers and smaller ships, it's not difficult to get around after a couple of false starts. But on larger ships, which seem *so big* on the outside, winding your way through endless cramped passageways and dead-ends can be a frustrating experience.

The decks are numbered from the main deck down. The main deck is the large, open part of the ship. Along with any raised, open platforms, the main deck is also called the weather deck. The superstructure is the part of the ship above the main deck. The "floors" of the superstructure are numbered, beginning with the 01 level (lowest), on up to the highest. However, on aircraft carriers, the hangar deck is considered the main deck, with three others (01 through 03) separating it from the flight deck. Decks below the main deck are numbered in descending order—that is, the second deck is just below the main deck, the third deck is under that, and so on.

It takes a while to get the lingo down. Men have been sailing the Great Ocean for thousands of years, so the new recruit has some catching up to do before he understands what the old salts are talking about. He will learn fast, if the chief has anything to say about it. He will learn his room is actually a berthing compartment, with bulkheads, an overhead, and a deck instead of walls, ceiling, and floor. He will not go upstairs to take a walk outside, he will used the ladder to go topside. Left and right will disappear from his vocabulary, to be replaced by the greater port and starboard, which is the ship's left and right, respectively, whether the sailor himself is facing forward (to the bow) or aft (to the stern).

The Plan of the Day is issued by the executive officer. It is, in effect, a "script" for the ship; it tells what will happen and when, from meals to movies. The POD is usually standard at sea, with some exceptions for out-of-the-ordinary events such as exercises and liberty call.

The plan will dictate the uniform of the day. The traditional "Cracker Jack" outfits with the Dixie Cup sailor's hat are actually dress uniforms, and are worn only on special occasions. At sea,

most sailors dress in dungarees, work shirts, and
"watch caps"—navy blue baseball caps with the
ship's name and designation stitched across the
front. The dress uniform looks outdated, but the
sailors love it. There was a minor revolt in the
ranks when it was briefly ordered out of existence
in favor of a nondescript doubleknit uniform that
made sailors look like bus drivers.

Most PODs call for a day split into seven sections. The two "dog watches"—four to six in the
afternoon and six to eight in the evening—are two
hours instead of the usual four-hour watches. This
splits up the day so that the men who draw the
first overnight watch aren't stuck with it for the
duration of the cruise.

Time at sea takes on a strange elasticity, in
which the days seem endless, but the tour is over
rather quickly. Most time is spent sleeping or at
work. On aircraft carriers there are all sorts of
diversions, such as boxing exhibitions, basketball
games, and "steel beach," a barbeque on the
flight deck, complete with steaks, volleyball, and a
band flown in for the occasion. On the few times
in the past when crews have spent more than a
hundred days at sea, the Secretary of the Navy
granted each man two cans of beer for his effort.

But such treats are few for crewmen on most
surface ships, although, to be fair, they tend not
to spend as much time at sea as carrier sailors.
Carrier duty is not welcomed by most seamen. The
ship is too big and impersonal, they say. Liberty,
if you get it, is apt to be cut short when someone in
the Middle East sneezes. Plus, there's the arro-
gance of the air wing personnel, universally referred to as "Airedales" by the ship's company,
although the term "aircraft characters," a per-
sonal favorite, is gaining some usage. Let's take a
close-up look at an aircraft carrier—and some aircraft characters.

Sailors in formal dress whites line the deck of *New
Jersey,* as it approaches *Enterprise* during VJ Day
ceremonies on San Francisco Bay. *Photo by Bill Yenne.*

Chapter Three

Carrier Ops

There *is* a door leading directly onto the flight deck. But rookies on their first visit to the aircraft carrier are never led through it. Here's why.

First, assuming your guide could find it—never a good bet given the fun-house nature of aircraft carrier interiors—the hatch is almost always secured during flight operations. And if it isn't locked, and you aren't stopped by the gang of deck dogs lounging in perpetual exhaustion near the exit, you are likely to walk out the door and into the whirring blades of two E-2C radar planes (and underneath the sign that said "Beware of Props and Rotors"). Or get clotheslined by the wingtip of an F-14 being slingshot off the waist catapult at more than a hundred miles an hour. Or be sucked into the intake of the voracious A-7. Or be blasted off the deck by a passing A-6, or blown off by an idling SH-3 chopper, or squashed like a roach by an S-3 slamming down for a landing.

No, too much mayhem. The flight deck crews live with such danger as a routine, but for a first-time visitor death is *not* a good introduction to life on an aircraft carrier. It tends to spook the surviving members of the media party.

Better to take them the long way around. They

Ear protectors and "cranials" — a leather and plastic safety helmet. *Photo by Michael Skinner.*

might have sneaked a peek at the flight deck as they disembarked from the COD plane or the helo, but to tell the truth, most people are so damned happy to be out of the noisy, stifling logistics bird you could lead them overboard and they wouldn't care, as long as they got rid of the cranial. The Navy says the cranial is a safety helmet, but in reality, the segmented leather and plastic thingamabob is a torture device to test how bad you really want to see an aircraft carrier.

Their first real look at the carrier comes after the cranials are pried off, noses are counted, and a short briefing is conducted. (Stay away from anything moving, humming, or squatting menac-

Opposite: U.S.S. Nimitz (CVN-68).

Spiral trim of the E-2C's radome is reflected in the bridge windows. *Photo by Michael Skinner.*

ingly on deck! Empty your pockets and sign this release! And don't look so worried—we haven't lost anyone in the three days we've been out of Norfolk!)

So the tourists step out of the hatch on the starboard side. Their first impression is how *high up* they are. The ocean seems to hiss miles below. It's as if they were looking down on the East River from the porch of a New York co-op. Their second impression is that the carrier is even bigger than they first thought. The island towers over them. That too would resemble a high-rise, if it were not for the antiaircraft guns sprouting from the second story.

But that's nothing compared to the shock the uninitiated get when they round the island. First, there's the smell. There is nothing quite like it. The scent of saltwater and JP-4 steam off the deck, a low, foul-smelling cloud that follows the carrier everywhere.

Then there's the noise. The place is absolutely screaming with jets. The roar of a cat-shot is more felt than heard. When an F-14 blasts off the sound pries through your open mouth and tickles your stomach. A carrier landing is almost as loud. Old hands say they can pick out the steel against steel as the hook hits the deck, but to most people a trap is just one big bash. It sounds as if the aircraft has crashed, which, in a way, it *has*.

Nothing prepares you for your first sight of a carrier during flight ops. Young men in wild-colored shirts scurry everywhere, barely avoiding taxiing planes, which, in turn, narrowly miss *other* aircraft, parked on every square foot of empty deckspace. Suddenly, the crewmen clear the deck, scattering like deer to hide among the huge planes that have somehow arranged themselves into neat rows. Their eyes turn to the stern, to a barely perceptible speck suspended on two columns of faint smoke. The moment is suspended in time. The whir of turbines fades into the background. You are dimly aware of some movement on the deck forward, but all eyes are turned toward the sky behind the ship, to the tiny, winged dot, barely getting larger as hours seem to pass.

Suddenly, the plane's shadow covers the deck. Then shadow and aircraft meet in a deafening smash. The plane tries to roar away, but is caught by its tail. There is a tense moment as the aircraft tries to escape, but it can't break the bond. Finally, the beast surrenders, the snare is released, and the ferocious fighter is led docilely back to the pack by the deckhands.

The drama is cut short by a new commotion, this one on the forward deck. Huge steel plates spring up behind another fighter. Steam is rising from a long cut in the deck. Workers are frantical-

Diamondback F-14 Tomcat launches off one of *America's* waist cats in the Caribbean. *Photos by Michael Skinner.*

ly trying to fasten the big plane to the flight deck. The deckhands run for their lives as flames sprout from the engines and the catapult engages. From a standing start, the aircraft blurs out to the edge of the deck and struggles into a starboard turn.

To the uninitiated it's pandemonium, complete chaos, but the flight deck has rules and rhythms more rigid than most human endeavors. Flight deck workers attend a short course called "P School" to find out how to keep from getting killed while they do their specific jobs. Here's a bit of what they learn, from the deck up.

The flight deck appears to be a solid, unbroken stretch of asphalt. Closer inspection shows it is actually steel, coated with a rubber-like material called "non-skid." Occasionally some of the grooved non-skid will work loose and find its way into the intakes of a jet engine, causing a major and expensive problem called "Foreign Object Damage." To guard against this, the entire deck crew musters in the morning, line-abreast, to march the length of the deck for a "FOD walkdown."

The flight deck is studded with white tie-downs, metal disks sunk into the non-skid about a yard apart used for securing aircraft on the flight deck. The white tie-downs are too small to be seen in most pictures of aircraft carriers, but on the deck they become the most prominent feature.

There are several other breaks in the seemingly unbroken deck. Several APU pits provide auxiliary power for aircraft on alert. There's an ordnance elevator near the island, used to bring weapons up on deck, and, of course, there are the Jet Blast Deflectors (JBDs), arresting cables, and catapults. More on those later.

There's also quite a fleet of vehicles zooming around on carriers. Some of them are quite large, but they tend to get lost on the five acres of flight deck. "Tillie" is an enormous movable crane.

Crewman's eye view of a fouled forward deck. During Cyclic Ops, launches and recoveries must be synchronized to the second. *Photo by Michael Skinner.*

(There is a hoist that is even larger called "Big John," fixed to the ship aft of the island, used to load and unload boats and aircraft when the carrier is berthed.) The "scrubber" is the carrier's equivalent of the type of machine used to smooth ice rinks; when the mixture of saltwater and JP-4 makes the deck too slick for safe landings, the scrubber is called in to clean off the ramp. P-12 is the latest, cut-down version of the carrier's crash truck. But the most common vehicle on the flight deck is the ubiquitous "stubby" or "mule," the squat aircraft tow-tug.

The flight deck is surrounded on both sides by a catwalk. There are seventeen fueling stations on the catwalk. Even-numbered fueling pits are on the port side, odd on the starboard. At the extreme bow and on the end of the angled flight deck there are extensions to catch the bridle attachments used by older aircraft for catapult launching. At the stern the flight deck slopes slightly. This is called the ramp, or rounddown. The dropline is a strip of brightly colored metal that extends from the ramp down the stern. It is lit at night to help aircraft find their way to the centerline.

The centerline does not run down the center of the carrier, but down the center of the angled flight deck, which veers to port of the car-rier's stern. Like the steam catapult and V/STOL "ski jump," the angled flight deck is a British invention, designed to allow the safe launch and parking of aircraft forward while recovery opera-tions are conducted aft.

The orange and white centerline extends down the length of the landing area, bordered on either side by the doubled white stripes of the safe launch line. Not coincidentally, the safe launch line is exactly as wide as the wingspan of the old A-3, the largest aircraft ever launched on a carrier. Starboard of the landing area there is a winding red and orange boundary called the foul line. Crewmen must stay behind the foul line during recoveries. Dashed lines by the forward catapults serve the same purpose.

Some carriers carry other markings as well. Helicopter spots are marked with circles divided by a line with a dot in the center. Spots one and two are forward, three and four are near the end of the angled flight deck. There is also a long, white arrow leading from the middle of the center-line to the bow to guide pilots to the correct taxi-ing angle after landing.

The centerline, dropline, and foul line are lit at night. The whole ship is bathed in sodium vapor lights mounted on the island. These "crime lights" illuminate the carrier without producing shadows. They outline the ship in three dimensions to pre-vent the flat, often vertigo-inducing "postage stamp" image of the carrier during night landings.

The most important features on the flight deck are the elevators, wires, JBDs and catapults. They come in fours, but that is where the resemblance ends.

The four elevators are the same size and power, but elevators 4 and 2 are used most often. EL-4 is the only lift on the port side (although the *Forrestal's* port elevator is at the very end of the flight deck, a bad place for it). EL-2 is the middle elevator on the starboard side, near the island. EL-1 is forward, but isn't used as often; it's fre-quently packed with aircraft during recoveries when the planes are stacked forward after landing. EL-3, aft of the island, is usually "tipped"—overhung with F-14s on alert.

There is a method in the seemingly haphazard way aircraft are arranged on deck. A seasoned carrier crewman can look at a picture of a flattop and tell exactly what was going on the instant the picture was taken.

"Cyclic Ops" is the name given to the schedule of synchronized launches and recoveries that enable the carrier to keep its planes in the air around the clock. It takes a lot of planning. Aircraft must be ready to go and arranged so that they line up on deck in the right order. Time must be set aside for refueling and rearming. The slightest delay can throw off the entire schedule.

The problems inherent in maintaining such a schedule are compounded by the peculiarities of the ship. Some of the older carriers have just two catapults. Even on the new supercarriers, with four catapults, Cyclic Ops can be stalled by bad planning or bad luck. For example, only cats one and three—the starboard catapults fore and aft—are watercooled. Only they can take the heat of an aircraft taking off in afterburner. In addition, cat four—the port catapult on the angled deck—cannot be used to launch S-3s and other large aircraft because the jet blast deflector is too small.

The Air Boss is the one who orchestrates the carrier's flight operations and must keep all these important details in mind. The "Boss"—or Primary Air Controller, to use his proper name—is the head of the ship's Air Department and in charge of flight ops. From his throne in the Pri-Fly tower, the Air Boss is the absolute ruler of everything that flies within five miles and three thousand feet of the carrier.

Crewmen called "handlers" help the boss shuffle the aircraft. From a room inside the island, the handlers, or "manglers," flock around a large drawing of the carrier's flight deck. Using metal models of the aircraft, the handlers keep track of the status of the planes on the flight and hangar

In his Pri-Fly, the Air Boss is lord of all he surveys. *Photo by Michael Skinner.*

decks. They keep in touch with the crewmen who do the actual moving via a two-way radio headset called a "mouse."

The carriers are plastered inside and out with "winged keys," the mark of the aviation boatswain's mate. These are the young men who labor on the flight deck and hangar deck to keep the carriers running. The hours are long, the work is hard and dangerous. These crewmen—most of them barely old enough to shave—are entrusted with a great deal of responsibility.

Winged keys are the symbol of the aviation boatswain's mates. *Photo by Michael Skinner.*

The Alert Birds. Pilots on Alert spend the afternoon in the cockpit. *Photo by Michael Skinner.*

The aviation boatswain's mates work for the Air Department, that part of the ship's company that supports the air wing's flight ops. The Air Department is divided into four sections: V-1 handles the planes on the flight deck, V-2 mans the catapults and arresting rear, V-3 is in charge of the hangar deck, and V-4 refuels the aircraft.

The flight deck personnel are further distinguished by the colors and trim of the jerseys they must wear on duty. The color scheme is so much a part of carrier ops that the flight deck workers are usually referred to as "shirts."

Hornet driver pre-flights F/A-18. The absence of a back seat and a naval flight officer has been just one source of controversy throughout the Hornet program.

Blue shirts are in charge of shuffling the planes on deck. Chockmen weighed down with chains and yellow wooden chocks trudge behind aircraft and tie them down once the planes are spotted. "Wing walkers" march alongside taxiing planes to watch for obstacles. "Plane pushers" do not push the planes by themselves; the white "T" on their jerseys signifies their status as tractor drivers. They man the tugs that tow the aircraft around on deck. A blue jersey with white trim indicates an elevator operator.

Aircraft captains wear brown. They work with the blue shirts, riding the brakes in the planes as they're moved around the deck. Helicopter captains wear brown shirts with red trim.

Visitors to the flight deck wear green jerseys. So do Marine guards and manufacturers' representatives (who have their own offices aboard ship). Plane inspectors—called "checkers"—wear green jerseys with white trim. Squadron maintenance officers wear green shirts plastered with squadron numbers. Most of the green shirts on the flight deck work on the catapults and arresting gear. They wear a black letter on their jerseys corresponding to the particular gear they're responsible for.

Crewmen in charge of the wires, cats, and plane handling wear yellow jerseys. Red shirts with black stripes handle ordnance on the flight deck. Red shirts with black letters are damage control crewmen. Purple shirts take care of refueling the aircraft.

The flight surgeon wears a white tunic. Medical corpsmen also wear white, with a red cross. Messengers wear a white jersey with blue trim. The crewman in the silver suit leaning on the crashtruck is the "Hot Suit" man. His only job is to walk into the flames of a burning aircraft and rescue the crew.

The aircraft on the flight deck have their own personalities. The F-14 Tomcat is the undisputed top cat on the deck. Even with its wings pinned back over the horizontal stabilizers, it is a huge airplane. The two dozen F-14s of the wing's two fighter squadrons are usually spotted aft on both the hangar decks and flight decks. The "Alert Birds" are parked behind the island. The two Tomcats are armed and fueled. F-14s on Alert Five are ready to go on five minutes notice. Alert Fifteen fighters take fifteen minutes.

Sometimes an alert aircraft called the "Deck Launch Interceptor" is parked on the catapult, its idling engines connected to the fuel pits. The DLI is ready to launch instantly, to back up other aircraft on CAP (combat air patrol) or scramble to intercept new threats.

The smallest aircraft on the carrier is the A-7 Corsair II. It's also the last single-seat plane left on deck (although its replacement, the F/A-18 Hornet, is also flown by a single crewman). There are a dozen A-7s in each of the wing's two light attack squadrons.

The A-7 is an aberration in the trend of heavier, more complicated carrier aircraft. The A-7E flown by the fleet does have a "cosmic" bombing system—there is an apocryphal story of a Pentagon study that showed it takes one-and-a-half people to operate the Echo's complex electronics, but otherwise, the straightforward "disposable bomber" is considered a real gentleman's airplane.

The carrier's main battery is the medium attack squadron of ten A-6 Intruders. The A-6 is constantly underrated by everyone but the Navy. Like the A-7, it is subsonic and not very maneuverable, especially when loaded with ordnance and fuel tanks. But the Intruder's ability to fly long distances at low level in bad weather with a big bomb load makes it one of the most valuable planes on the flight deck.

Tales of the A-6's bombing accuracy are legendary (but stories of Marine Intruders dropping eleven of twelve practice bombs in a Dempster Dumpmaster from three thousand feet should be taken with a gram of saltwater). At any rate, although the A-6 first flew in 1960, the design has been constantly upgraded. The A-6 is still in pro-

A-6 Intruders provide the real offensive punch of the carrier battle group. *Grumman photo.*

duction, with the new ones soon to be coming off the line boasting a series of major improvements, including the same engines used in the F/A-18. *John F. Kennedy* took an experimental all–A-6 attack wing to sea in 1984. The results were good. Look for A-6 squadrons to replace some of the A-7 squadrons that were supposed to be replaced by the expensive, complex, and short-ranged Hornet.

The A-6 design has led to a couple of highly successful spinoffs. There are four KA-6D tankers attached to the wing's Intruder squadron. These are regulation A-6s with navigation beacons and hose

E-2C Hawkeye traps aboard *America. Photo by Michael Skinner.*

SH-3 Sea King is spotted on deck. Rotors and rear fuselage are stowed to take up less room on the deck. *Photo by Michael Skinner.*

reels in place of the night and bad weather bombing electronics.

The EA-6B doesn't fire bombs, bullets, or missiles, but it's an integral part of the carrier's defense. And offense. The Prowler sniffs out and jams enemy communications. The EA-6B

The large S-3 Viking has an elaborate wing-folding mechanism. *Photo by Michael Skinner.*

is stretched to carry a four-man crew and sports more powerful engines to lift its huge bulk into the air. There are four EA-6Bs in each carrier air wing.

The E-2C Hawkeye functions as the carrier's AWACS, and is, in fact, used in that role by Israel over the Middle East. The wing's four Hummers are hard to fit on the hangar deck. They're usually spotted next to the island with the SH-3 helos.

The six Sea Kings, along with the ten wing's S-3 Vikings, make up the carrier's antisubmarine force. The S-3 has the same engines as the Air Force's A-10. Turbofans give the Viking the power to push through the thick air at low altitude (as distinct from the E-2C's twin turboprops, designed to help the Hawkeye claw through the thin atmosphere at high altitudes). The peculiar vacuum-cleaner sound the S-3 makes around the ship has earned it the nickname "Hoover."

Critical parts and people are flown in and out by the "COD-bird" (carrier onboard delivery). These are Grumman C-2 Greyhounds, the basic version of the E-2C Hawkeye with all the electronics removed. A similar stripped-down version of the S-3 Viking was used for COD duty between

Diego Garcia and the carriers off the Persian Gulf. The US-3, as it was designated, was never built, but the prototype still makes the run from Dodge City to Gonzo Station.

Carrier pilots adopt a superior attitude, not just towards the snipes and ship's boys below decks, but to everyone else in the sky as well. Air Force pilots are not known for their humility, but they are saints compared to the "boys on the boat." (The air wing always refers to the carrier as a "boat," which never fails to get a rise out of the ship's company. That's why they do it. The ship's crew can't complain—the carrier's skipper is always a pilot.)

The difference, carrier pilots say, is that USAF pilots are mere jet-jocks while *they* are Naval Aviators, scientists of the air. True, naval air training goes a little further into aeronautics than the other services, but the real difference is that USN pilots possess special flying skills because they are carrier pilots.

Consider the complicated and dangerous ritual Navy pilots have to go through just to get in the air. They emerge from the island, usually in pairs, chatting calmly, as if they could be heard above the crash and din of flight ops (style is important!). The crew has brought the aircraft up from the hangar deck, in a sort of naval version of valet parking.

After a cursory pre-flight—attention to detail would imply a lack of confidence in the flight deck workers—the pilot nonchalantly swings a leg into the cockpit and leans his elbows on the canopy rails. This is really to show plane handlers that he isn't going to hit some button that will let something dangerous fly in their direction, but the casual pose only adds to the naval aviator's image of icy-veined coolness in the face of coming danger.

The crew lines the plane up on the catapult with a metal device called a box. Once in position, the jet blast deflectors rise in sections behind the aircraft. The huge steel plates are designed to direct the engine's thrust up and away from the flight deck. There are four JBDs on most carriers, one for each catapult.

The cat officer gives the signal to run up the engines; one finger for a single-engined aircraft, two for a twin, slowly rotated. He checks forward and aft to clear the aircraft. A high-performance aircraft running up its engines is dangerous to be around. Wandering too close to the aircraft's snout will cause the poor unfortunate to be sucked into the intake and ground into sailor-burger (the A-7 is notorious for this).

And despite the JBD, anyone caught directly behind an engine running up will be blown off the deck like foam off a wave. Deckhands like to rehash the stories of comrades who have been chewed up, spit out, blown away, whacked in two, run over, decapitated by a passing wing, chop-blocked by a runaway cable, or any of the thousands of ways death and/or dismemberment lie in

Positioning marks for aircraft are spot-welded on the cat track. *Photo by Michael Skinner.*

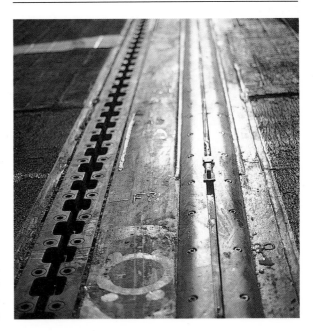

S-3 takes off on patrol. Carrier battle groups keep at least one Viking airborne at all times. *Photo by Michael Skinner.*

wait for the careless on the flight deck. It may be the giddiness of the survivor or the exaggeration of the young adventurer, but deckhands figure they lose at least one man a cruise. And this is *peacetime.*

The catapult shuttle—a device that looks like a roller-skate riding in the groove of the cat slot—is brought to the aircraft. Earlier carrier jets used a bridle attachment to hook up to the catapult. On later aircraft equipped with the nose-tow system, the shuttle is attached directly to a hook on the nosegear.

The catapult crew's hookup man jams the forward nose gear extension into the lip of the shuttle. There is another extension on the rear of the nose gear for the catapult "holdback." Holdbacks are color-coded according to aircraft type and weight. They are designed to break away at a certain level of force and keep the aircraft from launching without enough thrust to get airborne.

When the "hook runner" is satisfied with the setup, he pumps his fist up and down, a signal for the catapult officer to bring the aircraft under tension. When the pilot feels the nosegear stretch

under pressure from the catapult, he shoves the throttles up to full military power—maximum thrust without using afterburner.

The force of the catapult is adjusted to the weight of the aircraft; a catapult set to launch a fully-loaded Tomcat would probably fling an A-7 off the bow, never to be seen again. The more sophisticated cats on the newer boats use a computer to adjust the catapult pressure to the weight and type of aircraft, but on the older boats it must be dialed in by hand.

The weight is checked several times, although the aircraft is never actually weighed. Rather, the weight of the dry aircraft is added to whatever fuel and stores have been loaded on. The weight is important, not only to the catapult officer, but to the aircrew as well. If an F-14, for example, weighs out to over 60,000 pounds, it must use afterburner to get airborne. A cat officer holds the weight-board up to the cockpit for a final check. The pilot (or backseater in a Tomcat), gives a thumbs-up signal if the weight is correct.

When the pilot is ready for launch, he salutes. This is not always a regulation salute. Sometimes he only uses one finger. At night, the pilot turns the aircraft's lights on and off to signal he's set. A kneeling crewman windmills his arm and touches the deck in an exaggerated, theatrical motion.

That signals the monkey on the catapult, who puts up his hands (to show *he* hasn't touched anything yet), to check around the aircraft one last time. The pilot comes off the brakes and shoves the throttles out and up, into afterburner. The cat officer punches the button.

Nothing happens. The monkey doesn't actually fire the catapult. The button just signals someone below deck to fire the thing, so there's a three-second delay, the longest three seconds in aviation. In less time than that, the aircraft accelerates to 150 knots and is flung into the air.

Or not. If the catapult has not built up sufficient pressure to launch, or a nose gear collapses, or any number of likely accidents occur, the plane will dribble off the deck and disappear beneath the waves. This can happen in a blink. The crew—braced against the instrument panels with their fingers near the ejection rings—is often the last to know. The air boss is the first, and when he says "Eject!", the air crews eject.

Landing is no easier, or any less dangerous. In fact, "trapping" aboard an aircraft carrier is generally considered the toughest trick in aviation. Naval aviators like to think so, anyway. Zooming in faster than most motorists will ever drive, slamming down solidly on a space smaller than most suburban houses, snagged, and stopped. Suddenly. It's what separates the Navy men from the fly boys.

To help the planes get back aboard, the Navy has come up with a number of devices, none of which the pilots trust completely. The primary landing aid is a group of instruments—the Light Landing Device, the Fresnel Lens Optical System, and the Manually Operated Visual Landing System. Pilots just call the whole assembly the "meatball" because that's what it looks like. In simple terms, the pilot lines up the "ball" on his landing approach; the lights show if he's high, low, or in the groove.

There are also various electronic gizmos beckoning planes back to the carrier that account for a portion of the forest of aerials on the island of an otherwise lightly armed warship. And then there's the ultimate, the Automatic Carrier Landing system, a completely automated contrivance that will land the plane on the carrier all by itself in the worst weather. Even the pilots who trust it hate it. Nothing makes a naval aviator more uncomfortable than having no control, even if a machine can do a better job.

But the pilot's biggest landing aid is another human, the Landing Signal Officer. The LSO is always a squadron pilot, experienced in flying the type of aircraft he's guiding aboard. The LSO stands on a little platform aft of the port elevator, surrounded by safety nets. There's always a crowd on the LSO platform. Except during a bad landing. Then the air is filled with flying bodies diving for the safety net, a horizontal nylon fence that surrounds three sides of the LSO platform.

The LSO talks with the pilots via a headset. In his hand, held high, is a little switch called the "pickle." The LSO studies the pilot's approach. If he doesn't like what he sees, the LSO hits the pickle, the lights on the meatball flash, and the pilot has to go around again. This is called a "wave off."

A plane that attempts to land but fails to catch the arresting cable is a "bolter." The pilots aim for the third of four steel cables strung across the deck forty feet apart (although the older boats have only three wires to make it *more* sporting). The LSO grades each landing. An "Okay Three Wire" (with an underlined "Okay") is the highest compliment he can give. A "C" is the worst; the pilot barely got back aboard and perhaps should have kept going, had he known what was good for him. Somewhere between the two poles are "Tall Moose"—where the plane seems to slam vertically onto the deck, rather than gliding in on a slant—and "Into the pick-up," where the plane seems to climb *up* on deck from under the ramp.

Like the catapults, the arresting cables are set for individual aircraft and weights. The wires are connected to clever machinery below deck that manages to stop a screaming plane safely, without tearing its tail off or letting it slide off the deck. The inch-and-a-half-thick cables are checked carefully each day. A worn cable could snap in two under the terrific stress, and thrumble across the deck to injure or kill a crewman. If any flaw is detected, the wire is unhooked and thrown overboard. Even perfectly good cross-deck pendents are flung into the sea after a hundred traps, just to make sure.

The line between offense and defense is becoming blurred on the Great Ocean. The best way to defend against cruise missile attacks is to attack their launch platforms. And to do that, the carrier air wing mounts an Alfa Strike.

An Alfa Strike is an all-out attack on enemy ships or land-based installations. It is the carrier's—the fleet's—knockout punch. With the exception of the ASW aircraft and the minimum number of planes needed to defend the carrier, every available aircraft in the wing takes part.

Mounting an Alfa Strike is a monumental task. Just getting the planes off on time is difficult. Tactical aircraft can stay in the air for a mere hour and a half without refueling. If it takes too long for the strike to launch and form up, the whole mission is in jeopardy.

The flight deck is even more tense during an Alfa Strike; the pace is a little more frantic. Noise and stress are cranked up a notch. Loaded with fuel and weapons, the aircraft are more sluggish, harder to handle. They must be launched in a precise order. They must be launched without delay.

There are three groups in an Alfa Strike. The fighter escort will clear the way of enemy fighters and CAP the target. They may be directed by E-2Cs farther back or by a controlling agency aboard a Navy cruiser. On MIGCAP, the Tomcats will carry shorter-ranged missiles, the radar-directed Sparrow and remarkable heat-seeking Sidewinder. Navy pilots are proud of their reputa-

tions as dogfighters and are fierce foes in air-to-air combat.

The suppression group goes in first to soften up the defenses. The EA-6B leads the way, jamming radars on the ground as well as communications between enemy fighters and their controllers. A-6s and A-7s armed with long-range anti-radiation missiles try to pick off surface-to-air missile batteries. Their goal is to keep the defenders' heads down, to keep the enemy from firing at the strike group following.

The strike group is the carrier's Sunday punch. There aren't enough stand-off weapons to go around. Once the suppression group has fired their Harpoons into the target, the strike group goes in to finish the job. They can carry fragmentation bombs—which riddle the enemy's radar dishes and effectively blind him—and fuel-air explosives, which can create a monstrous fire storm and decimate lightly armored ships.

Usually, the strike group will carry ordinary "iron" bombs. The planes come in low and then pop up, to confuse the radars and give the crews a better look at the target. They'd better not miss; the low speed of the carrier's attack aircraft is a real drawback when trying to get away.

On the return flight, the aircraft will pass over a friendly ship. The ship will "delouse" the Alfa Strike, making sure no enemy aircraft are following the planes back to the carrier. Planes still carrying bombs will dump them into the sea rather than try to land aboard the flattop with live ordnance on board.

Of course, our ships can also attack their ships. And our ships can defend themselves against cruise missile attacks without the help of aircraft, although it's a tricky proposition. We'll find out just *how* tricky in the next chapter.

The "meatball" — a group of landing aid devices that are the pilot's best friend and worst enemy. *Photo by Michael Skinner.*

Chapter Four

War at Sea

When Lord Nelson sailed into harm's way off Trafalgar, he had no reason to fear anything above the sea or beneath it. Even as the French *Fouguex* appeared on the horizon, the admiral had half an hour to reconsider his bold plan. There was no need for rapid, secure command of the English fleet from *Victory*'s deck. The signal flags were sent aloft. The message was simple: "England expects every man to do his duty."

Nowadays, Nelson would not even have time to shake out his famous telescope. By the time today's threats appear, it's often too late to do anything about them. What would the admiral think of twentieth century war at sea, where missiles boil out from under the ocean, scream from the troposphere, or fly hundreds of miles under their own power?

Today's commanders don't even have the luxury of seeing their opponents. Even if the enemy were within sight—a possibility that grows progressively more unlikely as weapons' ranges reach out over the horizon—the captain no longer commands in battle from the bridge. Tactical decisions nowadays are made from deep inside the ship, in the combat information center. There, in the red-

dish glow of battle lamps and the ghostly green phosphorescence of data screens, modern skippers call the shots.

The shift from standing tall on the bridge to hunkering down over the video screen is indicative of the change in surface combat actions since World War II. The modern warship sails two seas: the Great Ocean, with its waves and currents, and the Sea of Beams, with its radio waves and electric currents. Like Nelson's wind, electromagnetic radiation cannot be seen. But it is the key to winning today's war at sea. Just as the ancient mariners used the wind to their advantage, contemporary warriors must ride the Sea of Beams to survive and win.

Modern ships attack and defend, for the most part, with guided missiles. Consequently, most space is given over to missile launchers and the electronic equipment needed to direct the ship's own missiles or confuse the "vampires"—incoming hostile missiles. Electronic warfare is important in land and air combat as well, of course, but it is vital in naval operations. Today, most of the ships' systems use the airwaves as their battlefield. "Hard-kill" weapons—guns, torpedoes, and depth-charges—are fewer in number but more lethal, as a result of electronic guidance.

A salvo from *New Jersey*'s 16-inch guns.

An aircraft carrier's island bristles with aerials and antennae. Electronic warfare is the key element in modern naval engagements. *Photo by Michael Skinner.*

The Soviet Navy is very interested in electronic warfare. The superstructure of Russian ships bristle with aerials, antennae, receivers, transmitters, bulges, screens, and various protuberances designed to fill the airwaves with signals that will find hostile targets and guide missiles toward them while simultaneously denying the enemy the communications he needs to press home an attack. The USN is also ready to wage warfare in the ether, but instead of relying exclusively on powerful transmitters and raw radiant force, as the Soviet Navy does, American ships tend to use deception and finesse.

The change from brute force to electronic firepower has changed the look of most navies. Gone is the heavy armor, the batteries of huge guns and smaller caliber weapons that characterized the old dreadnoughts. Post-war Navy ships carry only light composite armor to protect against fragmentation. Modern warships are bigger than their World War II counterparts, but the absence of great numbers of recognizable weapons systems make them appear less impressive. With their empty decks and sheer superstructures, they look like floating office parks.

But make no mistake. Today's surface warships

The nuclear-powered guided missile cruiser *Virginia* is one of the U.S. Navy's most formidable warships. But casual observers are often disturbed by the apparent lack of weapons on the deck.

The 5-inch gun is the largest on modern Navy warships. The Navy's lack of shore bombardment firepower was one of the arguments for bringing back the battleships and their big guns.

are deadly killers. Even a World War II heavy cruiser would have its hands full battling a modern frigate. Miniaturization has given naval architects the capability of putting the same amount of firepower in a much smaller package. And automation has shrunk the size of the crew, with the space saved given over to more fuel, ammunition, and electronics.

The higher rate of fire and better accuracy of modern naval guns has done away with the need for large numbers of duplicate weapons. Surprisingly, even in World War II engagements in which aircraft were not a factor—night actions, for instance—the smaller-caliber guns, with their high rate of fire, were more useful than the big-bore monsters (although it was the torpedo that usually decided the outcome).

With the exception of those on the recommissioned battleships, there are no guns larger than five inches in the modern Navy. And the majority of those guns are severely limited in their capabilities. *Perry* frigates—the most common class of warships in the Navy—mount a single 76mm.

An experiment that failed—an 8-inch major caliber
lightweight gun being tested aboard the destroyer
Hull. The gun proved too inaccurate and expensive,
and the plan was scrapped. *(USN Photo)*

gun, useful for some antiair and short-range sur-face actions, but of no use in shore bombardment. And the *Spruance* class destroyer's lone 5″ gun lacks the electronics and elevation to fire at air targets.

The Navy experimented with a larger gun for a while, installing an 8″ gun in the forward turret of the destroyer *Hull.* The Mk-71 Major Caliber Lightweight Gun was intended to give smaller ships the punch of a World War II cruiser. The first large-caliber gun designed by the Navy in twenty-five years, the Mk-71 was operated by a single crewman. It fired six different types of shells at the rate of a dozen rounds a minute. The

Phalanx 20mm gun firing aboard *America.* The six-barrel Gatling gun provides close-in antiaircraft on most modern Navy ships.

gun would have been useful in shore bombardment, but proved too inaccurate and expensive for Navy ships. The program was cancelled and the gun removed.

Surprisingly, with the rise of anti-ship missiles, some types of guns are making a comeback. Spewing out huge numbers of relatively inexpensive shells, modern rapid-fire naval guns can put up a "curtain of steel" between the target ship and the incoming missile, something surface-to-air missiles, with their limited numbers and slow rate of fire, could never do.

The Navy's Close-in Weapons System, the Mk-15 Phalanx gun, can put out up to 3,000 rounds a minute, using a six barrel "Gatling gun" arrangement. The 20mm shells are made of depleted uranium to give them heavy hitting power. The self-contained fire control radar is protected by a white dome. The resulting appearance, plus the gun's penchant for jerking into action seemingly without provocation, has earned Phalanx the nickname "R2D2" on board ship (although aboard *Enterprise,* which has three Phalanx mounts instead of the usual four, the guns are called "Huey, Dewey and Louie" after the robots in the Bruce Dern movie *Silent Running).*

Missiles are the main battery now, but guns are still useful for combatting the fast patrol boats that provide the bulk of Third World fleets. They're also good for "power projection"—electronic warfare antennae and missile containers impress naval experts, but there's something about gun barrels bristling on deck that makes people want to see things your way. Besides, as one naval writer points out, sometimes you need to fire a shot across the enemy's bow, and that's kind of hard to do with a cruise missile.

Modern warships cost more, certainly, but size hãs little to do with it. HY-80 steel is cheap, compared to the electronics that really drive up the price of ships these days. The cost of the hull is less than a tenth of the total price of today's ships. And America's role as keeper of the Great Ocean dictates that even the smallest ships in the fleet must be capable of blue water operations. A bigger ship makes for better seakeeping, as well as providing more comfort for the crew. As the Soviet Navy moves out into the deeper waters, they are discovering that the great many smaller ships they have built—though they may be the darlings of some members of the U.S. Congress—just aren't up to sustained operations far from port.

Paradoxically, bigger ships are, generally speaking, faster ships. In terms of speed, a large hull is much more efficient than a small one. In any case, speed is not the tactical advantage it once was. No ship can outrun a helicopter, much less a cruise missile. The Navy has settled on a speed of about thirty knots for entry into the carrier battle group. Carriers need a wind speed of about thirty knots across the deck to launch aircraft. In a dead calm they must provide that speed themselves, and the rest of the task force must be able to keep up.

Sustained speed is useful for steaming to trouble spots in a hurry. Rapid acceleration is useful for quick course changes in station-keeping and defensive maneuvering. Unfortunately, most marine power systems are good for fuel-efficient sustained speed or quick bursts of speed, but not both.

Conventional oil-burning steam turbines are reliable and efficient, up to a point. But to coax the last 10 percent of speed from the engines, an oil-burner will use the same amount of fuel as it does getting up to 50 percent power from a standing start. Since nuclear-powered ships also use steam turbines, they have the same drawbacks, as well as suffering from the poor acceleration rates of pure oil-burners. Smaller ships may use diesel engines, which are quick to start and quick to accelerate, although, as with steam turbines fuel consumption tends to go up geometrically with increases in speed.

On the other hand, there is the gas turbine,

which is really just a navalized version of an aircraft's jet engine. Gas turbines are enormously powerful and brisk. They can hustle a ship from zero to top speed in sixty seconds. Unfortunately, they are not fuel efficient, gobbling prodigious amounts of fuel, no matter what speed the ship is going.

To give ships some flexibility (and to give the world what it doesn't need—another set of naval acronyms) many modern warships are built with *two* sets of engines: steam, nuclear, or diesel turbines for fuel efficiency, and gas turbines for high speed, high acceleration maneuvers. COSAG stands for "combined steam and gas propulsion." The gas turbines are switched on to boost speed only when needed. This may seem wasteful, but it's actually more efficient than trying to run the oil-burners flat-out.

Some ships use different engines exclusively for different speeds. CODOG (combined diesel *or* gas) ships, for example, switch off the diesel engines and turn on the gas turbine for high speed operations. *Spruance* class destroyers feature a novel COGAG arrangement, using two gas turbines—one for high speed and another gas turbine engine geared for cruising.

Spruance destroyers need the extra speed for sub chasing. In itself, speed is not that important in antisubmarine warfare. Most modern attack subs can outrun all but the fastest surface craft, and at high speed the ship's sonar can't hear a damn thing but its own noise anyway. But at a dead stop, the sonar operates most efficiently, and the hunter doesn't give itself away. So ASW pickets use "sprint and drift" tactics, steaming far ahead of the main battle group, then crashing to a stop to listen for subs.

The *Spruance* is a good example of a modern, purpose-built warship. The trend toward specialized design was evident even in World War II, but most post-war Navy ships are built primarily to perform a specific role in a task force. *Spruance* is perhaps the best surface platform in the world for the prosecution of hostile submarines, but with a single 5″ gun and very limited antiaircraft capability, it depends on other members of the battle group to defend it from aircraft and enemy ships, just as the rest of the task group members depend upon *Spruance* to protect them from submarines. Critics can always find something lacking in every Navy ship, but the ships can really be judged only in the context in which they are designed to operate—as part of a carrier battle group.

The CVBG (aircraft carrier battle group) is more than the sum of its parts. Nominally, the battle group consists of at least one aircraft carrier and its escorts (although the Navy would prefer to go to war with two carriers in each group, to provide more flexibility in cross-deck operations). Usually a couple of cruisers stay close to the carrier. If the flattop is nuclear powered, the accompanying cruisers will be nuclear powered as well. About half a dozen destroyers and frigates—called "small boys" by carrier sailors—will surround the nucleus. They will be scattered for miles around in seemingly random positions, always moving. The exact locations of the escorts will depend upon the nature and direction of the potential threat.

Most important is the posting of the "shooters" —those cruisers and destroyers with long-range antiaircraft missile capability. If the axis of the threat is known, some CGs (guided missile cruisers) or DDGs (guided missile destroyers) will be positioned in that direction to provide a "missile trap." They'll shoot down as many oncoming aircraft and cruise missiles as they can, while giving a "heads up" to the ships at the center of the battle group to look out for any "leakers" that get through the outer defenses.

Some of the ships out on the perimeter can employ electronic warfare against the incoming missiles, to try to jam or confuse the radar seekers in the missiles' noses. Smaller ships can electronically enhance their radar image to appear the size of carriers to the incoming missiles. This is called

One of four gas turbine engines being installed in a *Spruance* class destroyer.

PROJECTILES AND OR ROCKETS MAY BE FIRED AT ANY TIME
WITHOUT WARNING. **STAND CLEAR.** NO UNAUTHORIZED
PERSONNEL ALLOWED IN THE VICINITY OF THIS LAUNCHER.
UNDER NORMAL CONDITIONS, A FIRING ALARM HORN WILL
SOUND PRIOR TO FIRING, BUT PROJECTILES AND OR ROCKETS
MAY BE FIRED WITHOUT WARNING. **STAND CLEAR.**

"banzai jamming," and is, understandably, not too popular with the crews.

Most ships also carry other countermeasures to thwart cruise missile attacks. Heat-seeking missiles can often be decoyed by flares. Radar-guided missiles can be misled by chaff—strips of aluminum foil ejected from cannisters that form a dense cloud to hide the ship from the incoming missile.

The Navy's primary electronic warfare suite is the AN/SLQ-32 (pronounced "slick thirty-two"). There are four different versions. SLQ-32(V) is the minimum EW (electronic warfare) set, designed to warn minor logistic and amphibious ships of the launch and tracking of hostile anti-ship missiles. SLQ-32(V2) provides additional coverage of weapons control radars for frigates and most destroyers. SLQ-32(V3) has the same capabilities, but gives the option of jamming the enemy radars. It's fitted to cruisers, some

Canisters containing chaff, metal foil strips used to confuse enemy radars. Chaff tuned to the proper frequency can simulate an entire aircraft or flight of aircraft.

destroyers, and principal amphibious and logistics ships.

Antisubmarine defense of the CVBG follows a similar, layered pattern. Although the Navy doesn't publicize the fact, there is usually at least one nuclear-powered attack submarine in each battle group. The fast attack sub prowls ahead of the task group to clear out any hostile subs lying in wait for the carrier. The attack subs operate more or less independently of the rest of the battle group. The surface ships would like more direct support from the hunter-killer submarines, but sub skippers are afraid close communication with the task group would betray their position and leave them vulnerable to counterattack. ASW

58

planes from the carrier and ASW ships guard the battle group's flanks against sub attack, while ASW helicopters from the carrier and choppers from the ships in the inner defense ring keep watch close in.

The ships communicate with each other through radio, or, in an EMCON (emissions controlled) environment, through flags and signal lights. In a fight, the most important communications network is NTDS (Naval Tactical Data System). NTDS consoles are connected via data link, so

Guided missile destroyer stands plane guard duty during flight ops. About a half dozen surface war ships accompany each carrier in the battle group. *Photo by Michael Skinner.*

each ship or plane so equipped sees the big picture. NTDS allows ships positioned on opposite ends of the battle group to exchange information. It's a real force multiplier, allowing each unit in the task group to see on its consoles what all the other units are seeing on their radar and sonar displays.

NTDS-equipped ships use a high-speed data link called Link-11. Ships that aren't patched into the NTDS network can still share in the information net using Link-11, but the data must be transmitted slowly via teletype, rather than appearing instantaneously on the consoles in the CIC. Large planes, such as the E-2C and the S-3, can use Link-11, but smaller fighters and attack aircraft are usually patched into NTDS by an ultra-high frequency voice link called Link-4A.

Depending upon the situation, the messages may or may not be encrypted. Data link is pretty secure, anyway—point-to-point microwave communication is hard to disrupt. But Link-4A could present a problem. The U.S. has put a lot of effort into scrambling communications between hostile aircraft and their controllers, and it's reasonable to assume the Soviets are also working on ways to jam or spoof such communications between our carrier fighters and their handlers.

To defend the battle group, the Navy has gone to a sophisticated air defense system based on vector logic. The outer zone is patrolled by F-14 fighters armed with the very long range Phoenix missile. With its sophisticated AWG-9 weapons system (pronounced "aug" as in "dog"), the Tomcat can track two dozen targets and guide as many as six AIM-54 missiles at targets up to sixty miles away. Midair refueling by carrier-borne KA-6 tanker planes enables the F-14s to stay on station for hours, or push their orbits out hundreds of miles away from the battle group. The E-2C directs the intercept, passing information one-way through the data link so both the carriers and the fighters can run silent.

In the vector logic system, single planes are assigned patrol areas. For every two fighters forward, there is another in reserve, ready to take up the battle if the planes on station are shot down, or run out of fuel or ammo. Behind that, there is *another* back-up plane on the carrier, in "Deck Launched Interceptor" mode. In DLI status, the aircraft is armed, manned, and standing by on the catapult, with fuel hoses connected and the engines running.

The vector logic system works better than the old outer defense systems, which were basically freelance set-ups, easily saturated. But unless the threat axis is well defined, vector logic takes a lot of planes, which is one reason the Navy wanted the Hornet so bad. The F/A-18 was sold as an attack aircraft, but its big improvement over the A-7 is its ability to contribute to the CVBG's air defence grid as a fighter.

Even in peacetime, carrier skippers put a lot of planes up in the air. There is usually at least one S-3 aloft, buzzing around the battle group snooping for subs. There is also an E-2C on perpetual patrol, even in the most benign environments. The Navy is *very* nervous about anyone getting close to the carriers. Task force commanders on Gonzo Station in the Arabian Sea have made it clear that they will open fire on any unidentified aircraft that come within five miles of the carrier at an altitude lower than 2,000 feet.

Any strange aircraft within hundreds of miles are intercepted, identified, and escorted out of the area. The carrier keeps two fighters, called "Alert Birds," armed, crewed, and fueled at all times for this purpose. F-14s on Alert Fifteen status are ready to scramble on fifteen minutes notice; Alert Five birds can get airborne in just five minutes. And in a really touchy situation, the Alert fighters will be constantly ready to launch in DLI mode.

The typical supercarrier air wing consists of about a hundred aircraft. Like the ships in the battle group, the carrier aircraft are specialized machines and depend upon one another for survival. In addition to the two squadrons of twelve F-14 fighters on board, each big-deck carrier totes

F-14 Tomcat refuels from one of the air wing's KA-6 tankers.

punch out. There is also a plane guard ship, usual-twenty-four A-7 attack aircraft (in two light attack squadrons), a medium attack squadron of ten A-6 bombers, four KA-6 tankers, four EA-6B electronic warfare aircraft, four E-2C radar and control aircraft, ten S-3 ASW aircraft, and six SH-3 ASW helicopters.

During air operations, at least one of the carrier's choppers will be airborne on "plane guard" duty. The SH-3 circles one side of the ship during launches and recoveries to get a head start on rescuing any crewman who may have to ditch or

Forward missile launcher fires a Standard antiaircraft missile.

ly one of the battle group's destroyers or frigates, on duty during flight ops. It may keep station anywhere around the carrier—except right in front—but it usually steams about a mile behind. The plane guard ship backs up the helicopter on rescue duty, and, once the crew is fished out of the water, circles over the spot where the plane went down to prevent the wrong parties from mounting salvage operations.

The small boys help the carrier in other ways, as well. They tow spars behind the stern for target practice. They try to put themselves between Soviet trawlers and the carrier. Sometimes a surface ship—usually a cruiser—will go in close to shore to direct flight operations ("Red Crown" was the controlling agency aboard various cruisers off the coast of North Vietnam during the war in Southeast Asia).

In fact, until the rise of the modern cruise missile, most Navy ships were relegated to protecting the carrier from other ships and planes. But the cruise missile has made just about every surface ship an aircraft carrier in its own right, and given offensive punch back to the black shoe Navy.

Cruise missiles are the contemporary equivalent of the Japanese *Kamikaze* planes of World War II. Each one is a small aircraft, carrying a warhead instead of a pilot. The USN pioneered the use of modern cruise missiles in the fifties with the Regulus program. But the Navy bit off more than it could chew with these early strategic cruise missiles—they were expensive and, ultimately, technologically unworkable. The programs were easily killed by the jealous carrier aviation lobby, who saw a potential threat in pilotless aircraft.

But the Soviets saw something different in surface-to-surface missiles: a way to get tactical air power at sea without aircraft carriers. The Soviet Navy went for these missiles in a big way and, after some notable failures, developed the weapon to a point that made even the USN take notice.

The Navy was late getting back into the surface-to-surface missile business. But unlike the Soviets, they've managed to come up with a workable weapon on the first try. American superiority in microcircuitry and small engine technology has made Harpoon one of the best anti-ship missiles in the world. The Navy now has more than 3,000 of them. It's an important program, but it hasn't received much publicity, probably because it has gone well.

Harpoon started development in the late sixties when the Navy needed something to defeat subs that might pop up close to the carriers and launch cruise missiles from the surface. But the missile has evolved into a potent anti-ship weapon, used by seventeen nations on a variety of launching platforms.

Since its introduction in 1977, Harpoon has been furiously backfitted to just about every USN weapon system on, above, and beneath the Great Ocean. On larger ships it's fired from ASROC or Standard missile launchers, although most skippers prefer the integrated container/launchers system in order to reserve more space in the ship's surface-to-air missile magazines. Submarines launch Harpoon from torpedo tubes in watertight containers. As it breaks the surface, the missile's first stage fires and it streaks to the target. Harpoon has been fired from nearly every combat aircraft in the Navy inventory, from the little A-7 to the big P-3. Even Air Force B-52s can carry Harpoon.

The secret to such easy installation is the missile's "fire and forget" quality. A smart weapon, Harpoon doesn't need an associated fire control radar of mid-course guidance from another platform. Give it a rough idea where the target is, and Harpoon follows a course set by its on-board computer until the target is close enough to be sniffed out by the active radar seeker in the missile's nose.

Harpoon has a range of more than sixty miles. To save fuel, it cruises at about twenty-five-hundred feet at slightly less than the speed of

Harpoon anti-ship cruise missile fired from canister launcher. Harpoon has emerged as one of the Navy's most successful programs. *McDonnell Douglas photo.*

sound. When the target is detected, the missile drops down to just above the waves. On its final approach, Harpoon pitches up sharply, making it difficult for opposing fire control radars to achieve tracking solutions. The altitude gain also lines the missile up for a near-vertical attack on the most vulnerable part of the ship. Harpoon's 500-pound warhead is set to explode only after the missile has penetrated the hull.

The much larger Tomahawk anti-ship cruise missile follows a similar course, but comes straight in without popping up. TASM, or Tomahawk anti-ship missile, is just one of a family of sea-launched cruise missiles that also includes the conventionally armed land attack missile (TLAM/C) and the nuclear armed land attack version (TLAM/N). With their long ranges—250 miles for the anti-ship missile and more than twice that for the land attack versions—the Tomahawks open up a lot of options for the Navy. But the opportunities are not without cost.

Tomahawks are expensive, technologically ambitious (more than half the initial test flights were failures) and potentially destabilizing. Although less than a quarter of the 4,000 Tomahawks scheduled for production will carry nuclear warheads, only the Navy will know which ones. The Pentagon thinks this is good because the Soviets will never know which ships are the real threats, and will have to defend against just about every Navy vessel as if it were a Trident submarine. But this could also tend to lower the nuclear threshold, if the Soviet Union decides to shoot first—with *their* nuclear weapons—and ask questions later.

The cruise missile has given the battleship a new

Tomahawk cruise missile fired from armored box launcher. *McDonnell Douglas photo.*

life. Armed with thirty-two Tomahawks and sixteen Harpoons, the battlewagons return as more formidable opponents than they were in World War II. Armor makes them slow, but it also protects them against the relatively puny warheads on most cruise missiles, which are often no more powerful than an 8″ shell. Phalanx antiaircraft guns and a helipad were also included in the retrofit.

But the main reason behind the comeback of the battleship is its nine 16″ guns, which give the Navy a much needed capability for shore bombardment. Each is capable of hurling a shell the weight of a Volkswagen more than thirty miles inland, although the old silk bags of powder charges threw off the aim of the big guns in Lebanon. The battleship can put 22 tons of high explosives on the beach with one salvo. It would take an hour for all the A-6s in a carrier's air wing to deliver as

Tomahawk long-range cruise missile during test flight. The long-range Tomahawk with its conventional or nuclear warhead has added great capabilities to the fleet, but has brought with it some disturbing political questions. *McDonnell Douglas photo.*

much firepower.

The reactivation of the *New Jersey* cost about $330 million, or about the price of a new *Spruance* destroyer. So far the Navy has gotten its money's worth, if only in publicity. Of course, it takes a lot less to run a destroyer than a battleship. *Spruance* needs about three hundred officers and men to sail. Automation has reduced the *New Jersey's* complement by nearly eight hundred, but the ship still requires a crew of more than sixteen hundred men, or about the same number as all the players and coaches in the National Football League.

But the Navy has found no shortage of volunteers to man their "new" dreadnoughts. The ship is not hard to run. Most of its systems are common throughout the naval surface warfare community. It uses standard electronic equipment, and its propulsion system is the same as that of the *Midway* class aircraft carriers, and the *Sacramento* class oilers.

Of course, battleships were not built with fuel economy in mind. The smudge rising from *New Jersey's* stack represents a lot of money going up in smoke. And even with all the huffing coming from the battleship's smokestack, the ship lugs too much heavy armor around for its old power plant to keep up with nuclear-powered carriers. Instead, the Navy plans to use the battleships in a task force called the "Surface Action Group."

The SAG is a throwback to the days of great —and flightless—fleets. The Surface Action Group (sometimes called the Surface Strike Group) would operate either in loose coordination with a carrier battle group or to escort an amphibious force or an underway replenishment group. Or the SAG could hunt other warships on its own, perhaps under the cover of land-based airpower or outside the range of enemy aircraft. With a battleship as the centerpiece, the SAG would operate with destroyers and frigates for antisubmarine and limited antiair protection. Armed with the mighty Tomahawk, the battleship could be used to strike hostile targets far inland. Such a mission could complicate life for enemy planners. But it presents some problems for its users as well.

Perhaps the toughest problem with using Tomahawk—and all cruise missiles, for that matter—is targeting. The cruise missile's biggest asset is its range. But that could also be its biggest liability. Targeting is not much of an issue in the land attack versions. Even the conventionally armed TLAM/C will be aimed at ports, airfields, depots—targets that aren't likely to go anywhere. Both land attack versions use internal guidance, constantly checking the terrain below against electronic maps stored in an on-board computer. And as for TLAM/N, well, as they say in the strategic services: A nuclear warhead tends to solve a lot of targeting problems.

But ships move, and knowing where your enemy is is just as important now as it was in Nelson's day. If anything, it's tougher to locate the enemy these days, because, with long-range, relatively slow-flying cruise missiles, you not only have to know where the enemy is, you also have to have a pretty good idea of where he'll be when the missiles arrive.

Target detection is perhaps the most difficult and most critical stage of modern naval combat. The side that gets the first shot has an overwhelming advantage. The days of ships lining up to exchange broadsides is gone forever. Warfare on the Great Ocean has become a series of ambushes, and the side that doesn't achieve surprise will most likely retire quietly. If they can.

There are two types of ocean surveillance: strategic and tactical. Strategic systems are concerned with the big picture. Both sides use satellites to keep an eye on naval bases and fleets at sea. American satellites are usually more accurate; intelligence snobs call Russian satellites "blob detectors." Satellites are still relatively invulnerable, despite a growing interest in antisatellite warfare on both sides.

And the data must still get from space to ships at sea. In the old days—say, five or ten years ago—satellite data had to be relayed from ground receiving stations to the fleet. By the time the commander at sea got the information, it was often tactically useless. Now, most major Navy warships can get satellite information beamed down directly. The Russians can do it too, but not as well.

Satellites have their drawbacks. They are scarce, fragile, expensive, and they can't be everywhere at once. Some in permanent orbit can be positioned to cover the globe, but it takes a while to complete the circuit, and they're apt to be out of position a great deal of the time. Some short-lived satellites can be launched for special contingencies, but they have to know where to look in the first place. In addition, the picture from space can be obscured by clouds and bad weather, and the enemy usually knows what the other side's satellites are seeing every minute.

Although the superpowers are working hard to improve their capabilities, so far there is no evidence that the systems have been refined to the point that enemy forces at sea detected from space can be *targeted* from there—that is, that the satellite itself can operate as part of a weapon's fire control system. So although satellites give navies a head start, they cannot be relied upon to pinpoint the targets. That's a job for tactical surveillance systems.

The USN has given the grandiose title "Soviet Ocean Surveillance System" to the rather motley collection of converted trawlers, aging bombers, ships, and subs enlisted to keep track of American forces at sea. The laws of the sea allow the AGI vessels to hound—and even disrupt—American naval movements in peacetime. And in the first stage of a surprise attack, the Russian warships shadowing U.S. Fleet movements might even get off the first shot. A nuclear attack by such a ship could have serious consequences, and it might as well be a suicide attack. As one naval officer puts it, Soviet ships will lead a "short, exciting life" in the next war.

But after the opening shots, Soviet naval intelligence would probably deteriorate drastically. Based on human observation and interpretation, the Soviet Ocean Surveillance System is likely to be overwhelmed by the sheer amount of data coming in, even as its sources of data quickly disappear.

The USN also relies on spy ships, among other

The Soviet Bear D, naval reconnaissance aircraft, shadows an American carrier battle group in the Pacific. The TU-95 is a common sight in the "Bear Box," west of Hawaii.

means, to gather intelligence. It used to depend on AGIs a lot more, but a number of American intelligence ships have been involved in rather ugly international incidents, which has inclined it towards more high-tech means of keeping track of Soviet naval movements: *Pueblo,* captured by North Korea in 1968, *Mayaguez,* seized by Cambodia in 1975, and *Liberty,* attacked by Israel in 1967 are examples. Some USN ships are still drafted into shadowing Russian exercises at sea. In fact, a guided missile destroyer, *Harold E. Holt,* did perhaps *too* good a job observing a Soviet V/STOL carrier dead in the water in the South China Sea—the Russian skipper fired flares at the destroyer's bridge in an effort to scare it away.

But the Navy prefers to use submarines for long-term snooping. There are nine fast attack subs fitted out for intelligence gathering, with extra sensors mounted on periscopes. The "Holy Stone" submarines are especially adept at keeping track of port movements and naval evolutions, but just about any American attack sub can be detailed to keep watch on the Soviets at sea.

The Russians also like to use subs for surveillance, but for tactical targeting, the Soviets, like the Americans, prefer airborne platforms. The mainstay of the Soviet naval reconnaissance forces is the TU-95 Bear, a huge, four-engine turboprop with long range and lots of room for electronics and fuel. In the war in Southeast Asia, TU-95s used to fly over American task forces as they crossed the International Date Line in the Pacific, just to let the U.S. Navy know they were not alone out there. It was a neat trick, but much easier to do in peacetime than in wartime.

The American equivalent of the Bear is the P-3 Orion. Designed as an antisubmarine aircraft, the P-3 has proven itself invaluable in the maritime reconnaissance role. It can also be armed with bombs, torpedoes, or Harpoon missiles, to attack the targets it has sniffed out. The P-3 is another example of a highly successful—and important—naval program that has not received much publicity because of its success.

But land-based aircraft have their limitations. They can travel long distances, but because it takes them quite a while to get to station they are not good for quick response. And, despite their long range, they have to be based *somewhere.* If there's no base nearby, they're useless; if there *is* a base close by, it can be attacked. The planes themselves are relatively defenseless against modern fighters and surface-to-air missiles. In fact, the only reasonable role for the Soviet Forger V/STOL aircraft is to chase away allied maritime reconnaissance planes.

Although land-based recce aircraft are generally more capable than their ship-borne counterparts, carrier reconnaissance planes are much better than

A P-3 Orion, the primary American ASW plane, returns from a mission keeping tabs on Soviet submarines. *Photo by Hans Halberstadt.*

nothing, outside the range of land bases. This is why the aircraft carrier is considered the weapon of decision on the Great Ocean. With its fleet of aircraft and helicopters, the carriers can search hundreds of thousands of miles, above and beneath the sea, and they have the muscle to sink anything they find, at ranges far beyond the reach of surface ships.

The E-2C Hawkeye has no equal in the middle of the ocean, keeping an eye out for long-range hostile airborne threats without revealing the carrier's position. The S-3 pushes the carrier battle group's ASW barriers out hundreds of miles. The Viking also has a secondary surface search capability that is getting more attention.

Most surface ships must rely on helicopters for over-the-horizon protection. Choppers have found a permanent home on all but the smallest ships. Their ability to take off and land vertically means they can be accommodated on board in very little space. And helicopters can hover, which is vital for prosecuting subs and spotting targets.

On the other hand, they are easily destroyed, slow, and short-ranged. They are no match for fixed-wing aircraft, but in the absence of carriers and land-based aircraft they can hold their own, as long as they stay low and out of the reach of enemy antiaircraft systems.

Target identification and acquisition is the most difficult problem facing naval officers today. The Navy is depending on helicopters for over-the-horizon targeting data, because cruise missiles

have no conscience. It's possible to get a fleeting contact, feed the bearing into the Harpoon and let it fly. Its terminal guidance will give it a good chance of destroying the target. Unfortunately, however, the target could be a neutral ship or another U.S. Navy vessel.

Sea weapons have gotten so sophisticated and long-ranged that positive target identification is a must. "Blue-on-blue" engagements—in which Navy ships mistakenly attack other, friendly units—are a common occurrence in naval exercises. This gives rise to a situation similar to air warfare rules of engagement, in which targets have to be positively identified before thay can be fired upon.

The new LAMPS chopper, the SH-60B Sea Hawk.

66

Helicopters can provide that ID, as well as mid-course guidance information for cruise missiles. But the chopper pilot must be careful not to make himself a target for the ship he's trying to identify.

The Navy is betting that a new system will help sort out some of the identification and targeting problems, as well as solve the big problem of how to protect the carrier battle group from attack. The Navy is betting a lot on *Aegis*.

In Greek mythology, Aegis was Zeus' magic shield, symbolizing his power and authority over the rest of the ancient gods. In the modern naval pantheon the carrier battle group is supreme—powerful, movable, and versatile. But not invulnerable. For the first time the carrier battle group—the Navy's Zeus—is itself in danger of being knocked out. *Aegis* is designed to shield the carrier and its escorts from saturation attacks by hostile cruise missiles.

Like Zeus' shield, the modern *Aegis* is built to dazzle and frighten its enemies. But it works by electronics, not the supernatural. *Aegis* is the culmination of nearly thirty years of tactical thought, naval doctrine, and high-tech engineering.

Aegis began life in 1957, in a converted garage outside Washington, D.C., where a research team from Johns Hopkins University's Applied Physics Laboratory was assigned to predict what war at sea would be like in the late twentieth century. This APL was the country's leading authority on naval surface-to-air weapons systems, having conducted the Bumblebee project to find ways to knock down the crude German anti-ship missiles late in World War II. That program led to the Talos, Terrier and Tartar missiles, and ultimately to the Standard series of missiles on Navy warships today.

The scientists dreamed a nightmare world, where hostile cruise missiles bore down on the carrier at all speeds and from every direction, converging on the battle group and overwhelming its defenses. But although APL's predictions have been proven correct, its first solution to the cruise missile saturation problem was a failure.

Typhon was their first attempt to thwart the

To silence criticism of its maneuverability, *Ticonderoga* cuts circles in the Gulf of Mexico.

notional cruise missiles of the eighties with actual fifties technology. *Typhon* was an awkward air defense system with a 150-ton radar array connected to banks of rather dim computers. Named after the ancient Greek monster with a hundred heads, *Typhon* was designed to counter an attack by up to two hundred cruise missiles. It was an ambitious program. Too ambitious, given the state of the art in electronics at the time; after three years of testing, APL concluded that Typhon wouldn't work.

But the Navy still had to find a way to protect its carriers from cruise missile attacks. In 1963, it came back with the Advanced Surface Missile System. And APL came up with a way to make it work.

Sea-skimming cruise missiles present a worse case scenario for most older antiair warfare systems. The missiles zoom in below the radar horizon, leaving the ship with less than three minutes to track, classify, aim, launch, and intercept an incoming threat. Much of that time is wasted as the radar antenna revolves—at least half the time it's looking 180 degrees in the wrong direction. More time is wasted as the air search radar data is handed off to the target illuminator, another radar with a shorter range but higher target resolution.

To deal with this, APL designed a prototype of the slab-like planar arrays that would eventually provide the eyes of the SPY-1 radar system. The arrays don't revolve the way conventional radar aerials do. They "stare" constantly, tuning thousands of time receivers to scan their sectors with a pencil-thin beam precise enough to pick up targets well beyond the resolution of conventional shipboard systems.

Critics suggested the Advanced Surface Missile System program was just *Typhon* in disguise, a feeling that grew stronger in 1970, when the program was given another name: *Aegis*.

It was obvious from the beginning that *Aegis* was going to be an important—and expensive—program, but the system had a long way to go before it would put to sea.

Congress and the Navy could not decide the best platform for *Aegis*. It was originally planned to mount the system on the forthcoming *Virginia* class nuclear-powered destroyer escorts, with a specially designed *Aegis* DGN to follow. Later, it was decided that the system was to sail on a conventionally powered destroyer. Two years later, plans were changed once again. *Aegis* would be installed on a nuclear-powered strike cruiser. The CSGN never materialized, and a year later an *Aegis* conversion of the cruiser *Long Beach* was put forward. The idea went nowhere, and in the late seventies, *Aegis* had come full circle, with a proposal to mount the system on a redesigned *Virginia* (which had since been upgraded in class from destroyer leader to cruiser).

A purpose-designed, nuclear-powered *Aegis* cruiser still has support in some quarters. It's probably not a bad idea, although an expensive one. Ultimately, it was decided to put the high-risk technology into a low-risk hull. The system was crammed into a *Spruance* hull, giving it excellent ASW capability, but the cramped design meant four arrays were needed for complete coverage instead of the two originally envisioned. The ship was top-heavy, despite Navy claims to the contrary. Eighty tons of lead were added to the keel and more fuel tanks were laid in the hull.

The resulting ship, much heavier and more capable than a *Spruance* destroyer, was reclassified a cruiser in 1980. *Ticonderoga* is the lead ship. The Navy hopes to build three *Aegis* cruisers a year for a total of twenty-seven.

Compared to most Navy warships, *Ticonderoga* is well balanced and packs quite a punch. Besides the two twin SM-2 missile launchers, the cruiser is armed with two 5″ guns, two Phalanx close-in Gatling guns, six torpedo tubes, eight Harpoon cruise missile launchers, two LAMPS helicopters, and state of the art, antisubmarine sonar equipment. All the systems are routed through *Aegis*, which automatically picks the best weapon for the target and the optimum attack pattern. The longer-range Tomahawk cruise missile and a vertical launching system will be included in future *Ticonderoga* class cruisers.

A similar version of the *Aegis* system will sail aboard the Navy's new *Arleigh Burke* class destroyers. *Burke* and her sister ships will perform for surface action groups and underway replenishment groups the same role the *Ticonderoga* performs for the carrier battle group. The *Burke* is a wholly new design, the first for the USN in more than a decade.

The *Aegis* ships will form the heart of the defense of the carrier battle groups. Its SPY-1 radar can track hundreds of contacts, with data so precise that the target need be handed off to a fire control radar only in the very last seconds of the intercept. Where older systems were limited in targets to the number of channels of fire control radar (usually two or four), *Aegis* is limited only to the number of missiles in its large magazine (and a further development will allow other ships to fire at threats *Aegis* has targeted).

The data from SPY-1 is processed automatically by the fifteen on-board computers that form the heart of the *Aegis* system. In fact, *Aegis* can be programmed to fire automatically when certain threat criteria are met. In the so-called "Armageddon mode," all the crew has to do is turn *Aegis* on. They can even leave the control room; *Aegis* will automatically shoot down anything traveling above a certain speed within ten miles of the ship.

Aegis uses a new missile, the SM-2ER (Extended Range). It's an upgraded version of the Navy's Standard surface-to-air missile, with some important improvements. It's a solid-propellant weapon, with an added fuselage section for extended range. The SM-2ER is also improved electronically, with mid-course guidance capability.

Combined with the *Aegis* system the missile can fly maximum energy trajectories, to get the most from its fuel load. Guided by *Aegis,* the SM-2ER

doesn't always have to keep its nose pointed at the target in a lead intercept course. It can "cruise" at the most efficient speed and altitude while *Aegis* keeps track of the target. When *Aegis* works as advertised, the ships aren't waiting for the cruise missiles; the ship's missiles are waiting for the target.

Since *Aegis* ships are designed to be the antiair command center of the modern carrier battle group, the combat information center on board is much more elegant than other contemporary CICs. The captain and other battle group commanders use four large multicolored consoles. The displays can be programmed to show an area more than two thousand miles from the ship, using information fed to the *Aegis* system from satellites, aircraft, or other ships. Normally, however, the displays are set at either 64 or 32 nautical miles, with another programmed at 230 nautical miles, the theoretical limit of the ship's radar range.

The highly detailed displays are just the visible part of the *Aegis* command and decision system. Using NTDS, data gathered by *Aegis* is instantly microwaved to all other units. They need not turn on their own radars and betray their position. The same is true of aircraft. *Aegis* can control a number of intercepts, relaying and processing information to and from carrier aircraft while the flattop itself runs silent.

Aegis has gotten a lot of publicity, most of it bad. The controversy stems from a series of early tests conducted on *Ticonderoga*. Their purpose was to wring the system out to its limits, and so to find potential problems before they arise. The Navy went looking for trouble and they found it; *Aegis* missed more than two-thirds of its targets.

The Navy attributed the problems to three causes: personnel inexperience, missile failure, and software bugs. The first of these was remedied as the crew became more familiar with the system —after all, nothing as complex as *Aegis* has ever sailed before. The missiles used in the tests were

earlier versions of the Navy's Standard missile. They simply were not good enough to keep up with *Aegis*. And the Navy says the last problem —software glitches—was easily fixed with a change in programming.

When the system was tested again, *Aegis* knocked down ten of eleven targets with the first missile fired. Even Pentagon officials say privately that those tests were little more than firepower demonstrations, but it's nice to be favorably misunderstood for a change.

The Navy is satisfied with *Aegis;* pleased enough, in fact, to gamble a great deal of prestige, money, and manpower on the most complex and expensive weapons system ever to sail aboard a surface warship. They say it proved its worth in Lebanon, where *Ticonderoga*—fresh from its shakedown cruise—accurately kept tabs on half the surface traffic and nearly all the air activity around Beirut. Task force commanders who had first been suspicious of the much-heralded capa-

The business end of the *Aegis* antiair warfare system: *Ticonderoga* lets a Standard ER (extended range) missile fly.

bilities *Aegis* brought to the fleet, eventually had so much confidence in the system that *"Tico"* was put in charge of the antiair protection of the American embassy and of the Marines stationed by the Beirut airport.

But the system's performance in the dangerous and confused situation off Lebanon is just a small part of *Aegis'* potential. Even the men who fought the ship off Beirut say they don't really know its limits. The Navy is only beginning to understand how to use the system to its full advantage.

Aegis has had to weather some rough seas. And it may turn out the system *is* a lemon. On the other hand, maybe *Aegis* will revolutionize war at sea. *Aegis* thinks fast, never blinks, and is always looking several moves ahead. Who knows? Maybe the Navy has an electronic Nelson on its hands.

The *Los Angeles* class nuclear-powered attack submarine *Salt Lake City*.

Chapter Five

Boomer's World

SLAP-slap-slap-slap . . .

It makes sense in a way.

Slap-slap-SLAP-slap . . .

After all, it's a big boat, but it's not *that* big. The Navy wants its men fit. And submariners are the most Navy of Navy men.

Slap-SLAP-slap-slap . . .

Okay, so he feels funny the first couple of laps, maybe. Or maybe not. By the time crewmen set out on patrol any moral scrimmage they may have felt about rubbing elbows with weapons of mass destruction has been securely settled. The Navy sees to that.

Slap-slap-slap-SLAP . . .

So around and around he goes, the soft-soled shoes smacking a rhythm on the hard, shiny floor. People on shore might grasp the instant irony of a man jogging to prolong his life around weapons capable of incinerating two hundred cities. But to the boys on the boat, the Trident missiles, slumbering in the twenty-four huge cannisters amidships—called the "tree farm" by crewmen—are just part of the furniture. He jogs on and on, past the weight pulleys attached to the launch tubes, past the exercise bicycle; sixteen laps to a mile in the underwater nuclear gymnasium.

Although the Trident is the biggest submarine the U.S. Navy has ever built, it is so compartmen-

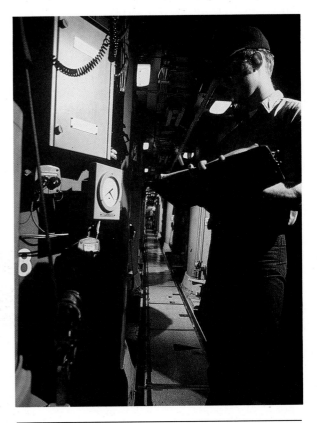

The lower ballistic missile compartment is called the "tree farm" by crewmen.

talized that crewmen see very little of it at one time. The crowded lower missile compartment would be claustrophobic to most people, but to the boys on the ''boomer''—the Navy's nickname for nuclear-powered strategic missile submarines —the ''tree farm'' seems as wide open as a Kansas prairie.

Of course, the scenery is much better outside. Three hundred feet below the surface, the sub churns at an easy three knots through giant canyons of breathtaking beauty. The pressure of the Great Ocean presses against the submarine, holding it suspended in the liquid blue sky. The underwater weather changes constantly. Great clouds of different temperatures roll across the depths. The sub banks gently, changing heading almost imperceptibly to take advantage of the cover the temperature layers provide against sonar detection. Still, he jogs on.

For getting away from it all, there is nothing like a nuclear submarine. Nobody on the outside knows where they are. Nobody. Not the Navy, not the National Command Authority, and certainly not the Russians. In the States, boomers leave port on the surface. Overseas, they leave submerged, with a tug riding shotgun on the surface to keep merchant shipping from bumping into the underwater sea-monster. The Soviet Union keeps watch on the sub pens around the clock; the Navy keeps twenty-four-hour tabs on the Russians monitoring the American subs. The game is soon finished. With a little electronic help from its friends, the submarine quickly disappears.

The routine of life on a boomer descends as soon as the ballast tanks are vented. The sub says goodbye to the world with a pair of claxon blasts and a brief bubble on the Great Ocean. For the next couple of months or so, the men rotate through a familiar cycle of standing watch for six hours and standing down for twelve.

Most of their time off will be spent in one of the fourteen ''rack rooms'' squeezed in among the missile tubes amidships. There, in one of nine

bunks stacked three high in a U-shaped design, an enlisted man can draw the brown curtain and shut out the rest of the undersea world. It's not much privacy by civilian standards, but to most submariners, sharing a room with just eight other men is living high—in some older boats, for instance, men sleep with torpedoes.

The officers sleep forward, in staterooms that are more luxurious only by comparison. All but the most senior officers must double up; some have two cabinmates. There is room for a desk and a washstand. As in the rack rooms, the officers' cabins are decorated with pictures of wives and children, girlfriends, or other remembrances of the world above the waves. But there is none of the permanent sprawl sometimes found in surface ships. There is room only for neatness.

Time sails by on patrol. Crewmen can plug into music pumped through the sub on an airline-style system that plays a variety of continuous programs

Exercising in ''Sherwood Forest'' aboard *Ohio*.

on four different channels tailored to tastes from Tschaikovsky to Cyndi Lauper. Videotape players have been welcomed aboard by submariners—*Das Boot* is a big hit with the crew.

Little things take on a lot of importance underneath the ocean. Meals are the major social events of the day. The Navy tries to keep its elite sub crews happy and, despite expectations, submarine food is surprisingly good, in fact has a reputation for being the best in the Navy.

Submarine life has some limitations, of course. Theoretically, a nuclear submarine could sail for years without returning to port. In reality, the length of the voyage is constrained by the crew's nerves and the amount of food they can lay in. The old World War II–era diesel submarines could carry, at most, three weeks of supplies. In some of the Navy's older attack boats, it's not uncommon for a sailor to have to inch through a passageway filled with crates of food during the first leg of the patrol.

The *Ohio*'s pantry is as big as the galley in some of those older boats. There's enough room for four months of supplies. The mess resembles a highway diner, but it is a palace compared to other subs. It seats forty-two in plastic and formica luxury. Cooks try to serve square meals, but if a sailor wants rollers and sliders—hotdogs and hamburgers to earth people—he can get them. Another gedunk favorite, soft ice cream, called "autodog," is a welcome addition underneath the sea. But the favorite meal among submariners is the Monte Cristo sandwich, in all its deep-fried variations.

Although there are a surprising number of diversions on the boat, most of the crewman's waking hours will be spent at work, on watch at his station. There is some physical labor on the Trident subs, but just about every one of the 16 officers and 137 enlisted men could rightly be called technicians. In some ways, these subs are more like an aircraft than a ship.

The operations compartment bears more resem-blance to a B-1 cockpit than to an older warship. In the sonar and radar rooms men stare at glowing scopes twenty-four hours a day. In the control room, the submarine's nerve center, the two helmsmen guide the boat with airline-style yoke controls. Back-seat driving is encouraged—there's even a metal bar between the helmsmen for the officer of the watch to lean on.

The men on board America's submarines are all volunteers. After passing rigid academic tests and security checks, they attend a two-month course at the Enlisted Basic Submarine School at New London, Connecticut. Most stay at New London for further training in their specialties before being assigned for a tour of at least a year's duty.

Crewmen responsible for keeping the submarine's nuclear reactor humming undergo even more training. Candidates for the Navy's nuclear field are picked out of basic training. They must be U.S. citizens between the ages of seventeen and twenty-four and willing to spend at least six years in active service. After passing the entrance exam and security checks, the candidate will spend well over a year in training at various bases around the country before he submerges for his first tour.

A lot of things the rookie submariner needs to know can't be taught in schools. The officers on board can help guide him, but the department heads are usually too busy to help with the day-to-day instruction; besides, in many cases, they are pretty new on the boat themselves. The responsibility for maintaining "the Navy way" underneath the sea falls on the Chief of the Boat.

Because of space limitations, the COB must perform functions that are shared among several chiefs on surface ships. He teaches the finer points of seamanship, keeps an eye on safety, and acts as the executive officer's right-hand man. He also assigns bunks and lockers and is in charge of supervising the cooking and cleaning details. Perhaps even more important, he monitors special leave and liberty, as well as supervising on-board training and enforcing discipline. The chief of the

boat wields a lot of power; a bad one can make for a miserable cruise, but a good one keeps things running smoothly as the time flies by.

There is hardly time to miss the people on shore. Civilians may tend to think that nuclear submariners spend their two- or three-month patrols loitering under the ocean, waiting for the word to push The Button. But there are a lot of things to do on patrol. The missile boats have two often contradictory objectives of patrol: stay hidden, and stay in touch.

The first part is easy. Modern submarines are big, but the Great Ocean is bigger. Strategic missile submarines are considered the strongest leg of the nuclear triad. The land-based silos are now vulnerable to attacks from new, highly accurate missiles tipped with huge warheads. Modern anti-aircraft missile systems make bomber strikes an iffy proposition. But the submarine, moving silently through millions of square miles of dark ocean, is relatively invulnerable to attack.

Once an American submarine disappears beneath the waves, it is virtually impossible to track. Both superpowers are working furiously on methods to reliably detect submerged submarines, but the oceans are likely to remain opaque for a long while, and to nuclear warfare theorists, this is a good thing. American antisubmarine warfare is far from perfect, but it is so much better than Russian means of detection as to approach destabilization of the balance of power.

There is even talk in the naval press about establishing "bastions" for Soviet strategic missile submarines, allowing them free passage through American antisubmarine defenses and establishing zones where they are declared immune from attack. The reasoning behind such a peculiar move is simple: the Soviets would be less compelled to *use* their submarine-launched ballistic missiles rather than risk losing them to the more sophisti-

Planesman and chief of the watch sail *Ohio* underneath the ocean.

cated U.S. ASW patrols. But there must be a better way.

Both sides are looking to outer space for more accurate and secure methods of strategic submarine detection. Infrared satellites could sniff the heat from nuclear reactors, or the hot exhaust from a conventional attack sub. Satellites sensitive to magnetic disturbances could pick out large metal objects, such as submarines, that disrupt the earth's natural magnetic field. Some could use an even more esoteric means of detection, measuring the almost-unmeasurable bulge a submarine makes on the ocean's surface as it cruises far below.

Despite the prospects of escalating the antisubmarine war to the heavens, sonar is likely to remain the principal tactical means of detecting subs. Some ships still use hull-mounted sonar, but most modern warships employ bow-mounted sonar, or the more advanced version, variable-depth sonar (VDS), to help isolate their own noise from that of the target. VDS is towed behind the ship, and is also useful for delving under temperature layers where subs hide. Most Navy attack subs are equipped with bow-mounted sonar, as well as towed sonar arrays, perhaps the most formidable form of tactical sonar. Dipping sonar used by helicopters is a form of VDS.

Maritime patrol aircraft drop "sonobuoys" —remote sonar sensors that relay their signals back to the aircraft via data link. Aircraft drop a pattern of buoys and work them for hours, as a hunter works a field of traps. They may also use MAD booms—magnetic anomaly detectors—for close-in work. With their mobility and relative invulnerability, aircraft are the best sub-chasers around, short of a dedicated hunter-killer submarine.

There are two types of sonar, active and passive. Active sonar is similar to radar. Sound pulses are transmitted through the water and those reflected back to the receiver expose the target. Active sonar does not depend on noise generated

Michigan leaves Bangor, Washington, for a Pacific patrol.

by the target, and is sometimes the only means to detect very quiet subs, such as modern diesel-electric boats lying low. It also gives range and bearing information accurate enough to launch an attack.

On the other hand, active sonar, like radar, tends to betray the hunter to the hunted long before the target is spotted. For this reason, active sonars are hardly ever turned on by Navy submarines. Passive sonar is much more widely used. Passive sonar is little more than a microphone stuck in the water. The ocean is a noisy place, so the microphone is connected to a computer, which compares the samples taken with a library of sounds stored in its memory bank.

American computer technology has allowed the USN to take the lead in ears in the ocean. The U.S. has a network of underwater passive sensors, called SOSUS (Sound Surveillance System), placed on seabeds around the world. CAESAR is the SOSUS installation based off the East Coast. COLOSSUS is a similar system off the West Coast. Other SOSUS sites are located in the GIUK Gap, the western Pacific, and the Azores.

SOSUS is a valuable part of the Navy's ASW effort. Although it is apparently not accurate enough to pinpoint hostile submarines exactly, it drastically cuts down on the area antisubmarine assets must search, giving them a headstart in finding the needle in the underwater haystack. Some estimates say SOSUS can narrow down a search area to as little as thirty miles. The Soviets realize the value of the SOSUS systems. They've even started to deploy a similar, though not as capable, system of their own. But in a war with the U.S. they'd be more concerned with disabling the fragile American system.

The Navy is building a back-up for the SOSUS system. SURTASS (Surveillance Towed Array System) is an array of acoustic sonars hauled around by a tugboat. In peacetime, SURTASS fills gaps in the SOSUS systems and provides a closer look. In war, it could replace "permanent" sites that prove less than permanent.

Sonar systems, especially the new American versions, are growing ever more complex. Connected to giant computers, they can instantly match noises and targets, sometimes to distances ranging hundreds of miles. But there are a number of factors that can seriously degrade sonar performance. And sub skippers use every trick in the book to stay hidden.

Since sound vibrations, like radar waves, travel in a straight line, subs hide among underwater mountain ranges and ice packs to put a barrier between themselves and the sensor. As we have mentioned, they can hide in layers of water that are colder or warmer than the surrounding sea, causing a distortion of the sonar waves. Temperature variation is most pronounced when surface water is heated by the sun. The so-called "afternoon effect" drastically reduces sonar range by bending the sound waves downward.

Salinity and water pressure affect sonar performance as well. Knowing the underwater weather forecast is important enough for the sub captains to risk detection by sending a thermobuoy to the surface. The buoy sends the temperature of the various layers back to the sub. On its way up, the thermobuoy could very well pass another thermobuoy on its way down sent by a surface ship.

Perhaps the most effective means of escaping detection is not to make any noise. This is more difficult than it sounds. Even nuclear submarines can be betrayed by the noise made by water being pumped through the reactor cooling system. Subs powered by diesel-electric power make no such noise operating on batteries. For this reason, they are very, very quiet, skulking at the bottom with all power stopped.

Of course, the faster a submarine travels, the more noise it makes. This is not only due to the racket of the engines, but to a phenomenon known as "cavitation noise", the circular wake of air bubbles and disturbed water churned up by the sub's propeller. So although modern submarines are easily as fast as most surface ships, they use their top speed only in emergencies.

Whenever possible, the subs try to mask their noise through proximity with other, louder sounds. Submariners love whales; ASW hunters do not. Whales can be heard for hundreds of miles, especially when they're in a romantic mood. Offshore oil rigs are also favorite noise-makers. And subs will often hide underneath noisy freighters, especially when they must traverse busy sections of the Great Ocean.

Once they reach their patrol area, the boomers usually cruise about as fast as a man can walk. They're in no hurry. They've got nowhere to go. Besides, the quieter they are, the better they hear. They are silent, listening very hard. They hear the hunters hundreds of miles away, scrambling through the underwater underbrush. They slip silently away, like Indians.

In fact, if the nuclear subs didn't have to communicate with the outside world, they could probably never be found. But it is vital that they stay in contact to accomplish their mission. Sub skippers are very careful how they touch base—it's the touchiest part of any patrol. The boomers have a variety of methods to stay in touch. Unfortunately, none of them is foolproof, and all of them drastically increase the danger of detection.

Subs hardly ever use periscopes anymore. A periscope-mounted radar is sometimes useful to spot ASW search planes, but if the aircraft spots the antenna on his radar, it just makes his job easier (radar-absorbing materials reportedly used in the Stealth projects were pioneered as coatings for sub periscopes). Spy submarines have various electronic warfare antenna mounted on periscopes

78

Ohio prior to precommissioning ceremonies.

to snoop on enemy exercises, but it's usually too risky for regular subs to come to periscope depth just for the luxury of visual sightings.

Subs also have a microwave dish that receives messages from defense satellites. It's the best way to pick up complex messages, but since at least part of the sub has to break the surface to use it, microwave communication is also asking for it. In peacetime, though, peeking out from the waves for a brief burst of satellite telemetry is not so critical. The fifty-word coded messages for each crewman on patrol are probably transmitted via satellite. The eight "family grams" are their only contact with the outside world.

The Navy has tried a number of schemes using extremely low frequency waves to communicate with their missile boats. ELF systems set up a giant radio circuit using the earth to complete the loop. The resulting waves are powerful enough to cover the globe, even to great underwater depths. They are also slow. It takes an hour to send a dozen letters, an hour and fifteen minutes just to say "Trident Submarine."

Or the subs can send up a radio buoy. This is no more than a tape recorder and a transmitter sent to the surface. Of course, the radio buoy's transmission would reveal its position, but a time delay could be introduced so that by the time it started

broadcasting, the sub would be long gone. The problem is that the message only goes one way, and the captain can't be sure it's been received.

The sub can receive messages from NEACAP (the National Emergency Airborne Command Post, or "Flying White House"), or, as a last-ditch maneuver, the Emergency Rocket Communication System, a Minuteman missile armed not with a warhead, but a radio transmitter. If all other command centers have been decimated, ERCS will screech through the sky, beeping its doomsday launch message to anyone still alive to hear it.

But if worse comes to worst, the boomers will probably get The Word from TACAMO, the "Take Charge and Move Out" aircraft constantly aloft over the Great Ocean. The old TACAMO birds are highly modified C-130s, but the Navy is getting a new burglar alarm in the form of the E-6, yet another variation of the Boeing 707/C-135 airframe. The E-6 trails an antenna five miles long, communicating with the submerged sub, trailing a long antenna of its own. The messages cannot be too complicated. But then, they don't have to be.

The press was shocked recently when a Navy admiral revealed that, under certain circumstances, submarine crews can launch their missiles without confirmation from the outside world. But given the difficulty inherent in communicating with submerged submarines and their role as a last resort, it would be surprising if they could not. However, any launch requires the cooperation of nearly all the one-hundred-fifty-odd men on board, all volunteers, constantly checked for cracks, so a renegade launch is not a likely event.

Still, it is an enormous responsibility. The gold and blue crews of America's silent service have conducted more than two thousand strategic deterrent patrols since the introduction of the Navy's first ballistic missile submarine nearly twenty-five years ago. Their record is unblemished. Working autonomously in a high-pressure world where so many things could go seriously wrong, nothing

has. Ever. It's a tribute to the more than two thousand naval officers serving aboard submarines at sea.

The order to launch would come in the form of an Emergency Action Message. The captain checks the coded transmission with a message stashed in his safe. If it matches, it's a go launch.

The crew constantly practices launches. In the mission control room, enlisted men lean over consoles with row after row of brightly colored buttons. But the button that really counts is kept locked; it's on a pistol grip at the end of a long, coiled cord.

If the weapons officer pushes that button, gas and steam will fill the launch tube. The missile will be punched out by enormous pressure until it breaks the surface, where the first stage will fire and send the missile on its way. Meanwhile, the tube will fill up with water, providing ballast to steady the sub. The next missile is now ready to fire. The whole operation takes less than a minute.

The two dozen Trident C-4 ballistic missiles wait in suspended animation, each tipped with eight nuclear warheads that can be targeted individually. With the touch of a button, each Trident submarine can wipe out nearly two hundred

Here's Boomer! *Ohio* (SSBN-726), lead ship of the class of largest American submarines ever built.

targets four thousand miles away. But the Trident C-4 is not the last word in submarine-launched ballistic missiles. Beginning in 1989, the new *Ohio*s will carry the even more potent Trident D-5, with all subs in the class eventually slated for the upgrade.

Lafayette class ballistic missile sub *James K. Polk* (SSBN-645). The *Lafayette* boats are still the largest class in the strategic missile deterrent force.

79

Los Angeles class nuclear-powered attack sub *Birmingham* surfaces for the camera. While on patrol, nuclear-powered subs surface only for emergencies.

In the metaphysics of nuclear warfare, the D-5 is a more "humane" weapon. More powerful and more accurate than the old "city-busters," the D-5 can be used in pinpoint attacks against targets such as hardened missile silos. That also makes it more destabilizing. Up till now, submarine-launched ballistic missiles have been too short-ranged and inaccurate to be considered "first-strike" weapons. They lacked the third stage of land-based intercontinental missiles. Moreover, the movement of the submarine—and thus the missile's launch point—introduced an element of uncertainty into the missile's inertial guidance system.

But the Trident D-5 is the first submarine-launched missile that can be called a "counter-force" weapon. The largest such missile ever fielded by the U.S., the three-stage D-5 has a range of more than four thousand miles. And it can hit targets within a twelve-hundred-foot circle, owing to a new guidance system that checks the warhead's position against stars in space.

The $2 billion *Ohio* subs are as big as cruisers. Construction of a dozen of the giant strategic missile subs has been authorized. More are probably on their way. The ships are built at the rate of about one a year, to avoid block obsolescence.

Along with thirty-one older *Lafayette* class Poseidon subs, the *Ohio* boats form the undersea leg of the American nuclear triad. The Navy's boomers carry five thousand warheads, more than half the nuclear warheads in the American strategic arsenal. Although the terms Trident sub and *Ohio* class sub are usually considered synonymous, the last dozen *Lafayette*s have also been converted to fire the Trident missile.

Displacing more than eighteen thousand tons, the 560-foot-long *Ohio* is the largest American submarine ever built. But it is not the largest submarine in the world. That distinction belongs to the Soviet *Typhoon* class ballistic missile submarine, reportedly nearly ten thousand tons larger than the *Ohio* class subs.

Typhoon is larger than the Washington Monument. Although it carries fewer missiles than the *Ohio* subs, it represents a dangerous development in Soviet strategic missile submarine warfare. *Typhoon* skippers can jam the sub up against an ice pack, hiding among the floe's downward peaks in a maneuver called the "ice pick." The submarine can skulk there, motionless, for months at a time. There is even evidence that the new Soviet submarines can launch their missiles *through* the ice. If this is true, it is bad news for the Navy. If *Typhoon* doesn't have to come out to fight, it might not be found until it's too late.

The Soviet Navy is very much a submarine force. Their impressive new surface ships get a lot of attention, but the Russians have always concentrated on submarines. They already outnumber the United States three-to-one under the Great Ocean. But their underwater order of battle contains a great many diesel-electric patrol submarines, a type of U-boat the USN says it has no use for. Furthermore, Soviet subs are no match for American boats, one-on-one. They're noisy, relatively unsophisticated, and don't carry a great number of weapons reloads.

Nevertheless, in terms of sheer numbers, the Soviet Navy is the world's most powerful submarine force. They've got almost twice as many strategic missile submarines, and nearly three times as many attack boats. And in the last decade, the Soviets have introduced a dozen classes of submarines, including two brand-new nuclear attack boats, the *Mike* and *Sierra* classes.

To counter growing Soviet strength under the ocean, the USN is relying more and more on its fleet of nuclear attack submarines. In time of war, the attack boats will operate independently, against both surface and sub-surface targets, either clearing a path for carrier battle groups and convoys or striking out on their own on hunter-killer missions deep in enemy territory. There has been a recent emphasis on coordinating the operations of the Navy's attack submarines more

closely with the carrier task forces, but they share the boomers' problems with secure, two-way communications.

The backbone of the American attack sub fleet is the *Los Angeles* class submarine. The Russians have some subs that dive deeper or go faster. But in the qualities that really count in an attack submarine—stealth, endurance, and firepower— the *Los Angeles* class sub is the best in the world. The Navy has more than forty of them, and with plenty more called for in Navy plans, the *Los Angeles* class is the largest class of nuclear submarines built by any nation.

The *Los Angeles* subs are two hundred feet shorter and nearly ten thousand tons lighter than the *Ohio*s. With only slightly fewer men on board, they are more crowded. The layout is roughly the same. The bow is taken up by the huge sonar dome, connected to the rest of the boat by a passageway that runs through the forward ballast tanks. Next come the four torpedo tubes, canted outward, followed by the adjacent torpedo room.

Above are crew's quarters and, below the sail, the attack center, with sonar and radar rooms. Underneath are storage batteries and auxiliary machinery. The rest of the boat is taken up by the reactor and the engine room, with the aft ballast tanks surrounding the propeller shaft.

Navy attack submarines get the drop on their prey through information gathered by SOSUS or defense satellites that monitor Soviet subs as they leave port. Sometimes the subs are part of the information net themselves, lying low in waters close to the Soviet Union, cataloging the acoustic signatures of boats passing by. A boomer will sneak away silently if it detects someone in the neighborhood; the captain of an attack submarine will probably close with the intruder for an unscheduled (and rather one-sided) war game.

The attack submarine's principal weapon is the Mk-48 torpedo, a twenty-foot long, 3,500 pound,

olive drab monster guided to the target by signals generated by the Mk-117 fire control system. The Mk-117 takes fixes from the bow-mounted sonar and the towed array. The triangulation helps pinpoint the target. Target information is fed to the torpedo via a long, thin strand of wire. The Mk-48 bangs out of the tube and heads for the target at speeds up to a mile a minute. Long before it reaches the limits of its advertised range of over thirty miles, the wire will snap and the torpedo will guide itself to the target using its on-board sonar.

A typical tactic is to fire torpedoes in salvoes of two. One fish runs at top speed, noisy and easily detected. The other torpedo runs quietly at slower speed. As the enemy sub turns to avoid the first torpedo, the other Mk-48 bores in undetected.

More than likely, the attack submarine skipper won't know if the torpedo hit the target. He's got to go. The noisy torpedo, screwing through the ocean, has announced his presence. Everyone now knows where he *was.* Now he's got to be somewhere else, or *he'll* be the target.

The Navy has recently expressed some concern over the effectiveness of their torpedoes. Specifically, it's thought that the Soviet *Alfa* class submarine could, in some cases, outrun or outfox the Navy's current inventory of undersea weapons.

The *Alfa* is an ambitious design, with no equal in the West. It is extremely fast, once clocked at forty-three knots by an American attack submarine that was attempting to trail it underwater. The *Alfa* has a revolutionary titanium hull that allows it to dive deeper than other subs, and use deeper temperature gradients and ocean floor topography for concealment. The hull is coated with a Clusterguard anti-sonar coating that makes it difficult to detect.

On the other hand, as is the case with most dreaded Russian hardware, there is evidence that the *Alfa* boats are not the sea monsters first feared

Attack center of *La Jolla, Los Angeles* class attack sub.

by Navy planners. The subs have never been put in serial production. There could be problems in producing the ambitious design. Or it could be the *Alfa* is merely a technology demonstrator. There are reports of serious problems concerning the sub's nuclear power plant. And the much-vaunted Clusterguard coating tends to come unstuck, flapping in the water, making the sub easier, not harder, to detect.

Still, the Navy is worried about the *Alfa*'s potential, if nothing else. The Mk-48 is undergoing an advanced capability program (ADCAP), that will improve its depth and speed performance. The Mk-46 lightweight torpedo, carried on some ships, aircraft, and helicopters, is being upgraded to make its sonar guidance system less susceptible to countermeasures. In the long run, the Mk-46 will be replaced by a new, lightweight torpedo, the Mk-50, which will reportedly use a directed-energy warhead and will be effective against surface ships and even diesel subs in shallow waters.

Some U.S. attack subs also carry SUBROC, a rocket-powered depth charge similar to the ASROC carried by surface ships. SUBROC will be replaced by the new ASWSOW (antisubmarine warfare stand-off weapon) under development, with improved range and guidance. The whole family of depth charges is armed with nuclear warheads, which makes them very effective when hunting high-value targets such as enemy ballistic missile submarines. But they raise some problems of their own. Nuclear weapons require the type of authorization not easily transmitted to submarines trying to keep a low profile.

Nevertheless, many naval experts feel the first use of nuclear weapons will be at sea. They're the best way to bag a carrier (or sneaky submarines). Saltwater is an excellent medium in which to diffuse radiation. And there are no civilian targets in the middle of the Great Ocean, hence no collateral damage. Or, as one Navy man puts it: "You can't blow a hole in the ocean."

Navy attack submarines aren't built for attacking surface ships. Russian boomers are their primary targets, plus any enemy attack boats that get in the way. Their weapons are primarily designed for ASW. In fact, the Argentine cruiser

sunk by the British nuclear sub in the Falklands was sent to the bottom by World War II–era torpedoes.

Soviet Oscar-class nuclear-powered cruise attack sub.

The Navy is now re-thinking the role of nuclear attack subs against surface ships. They're putting new missiles in the subs. Both the Harpoon and Tomahawk cruise missiles were designed to be fired from torpedo tubes. Each is capable of surface attack, although over-the-horizon guidance will be a problem with the Tomahawk, as it is with all long-range cruise missiles.

Another problem is weapons load-out. The subs are crowded enough as it is, and there's not much room for more weapons in the torpedo rooms. Even the biggest boats can't carry more than twenty Mk-48s. Also, there are only four tubes, so the skipper has to anticipate which weapons —torpedoes, SUBROC, Harpoons, Tomahawks, or mines—will be needed, and in which order. Some of these problems will be resolved when *Los Angeles* class subs are built with a dozen dedicated Tomahawk vertical launch tubes installed outside the pressure hull.

The *Los Angeles* class will be America's primary attack submarine until the turn of the century. But looming block obsolescence of the earlier *Permit* and *Sturgeon* attack submarine classes, as well as the relentless pursuit of submarine technology on the part of the Soviet Union, has led Navy brass to investigate the design of a new nuclear attack submarine for the twenty-first century.

Dubbed the SSN-21, the new sub, in the words of a senior Navy official, will be "the most heavily armed, the fastest, the deepest-diving, most combat-capable submarine ever built." The first SSN-21 will sail in about ten years.

American control of the under-oceans should survive until then. The Soviet Union is working hard to close the gap, putting forth great technical effort of their own, in addition to "borrowing" the best from the West. But the Silent Service remains silent where it counts. Says a high-ranking naval officer, "We can detect their submarines before they detect ours." And that's what it's all about.

Chapter Six

The Other U.S. Navies

It's no secret that the Navy is divided into three "unions": the surface warfare, submarine, and naval air communities. Isolated training tracks begin the division. Competition for funds available in a limited budget accentuates it. Each community is all for a combined arms approach in the abstract, but when it comes down to it, they feel *theirs* is the decisive weapon in combat. And they're not shy about letting everyone else know.

What gets lost in the shuffle of the brown shoes versus black shoes (and aviation boots) is all the vital, but little publicized, missions a modern Navy must carry out.

First of all, a modern Navy must be supplied. This is hard enough in port, but when ships stay on station months at a time, supply lines must be extended to the ships at sea. The Navy does this with underway replenishment. The majority of ships in the Navy are such supply vessels and their bodyguards. Some are detailed for convoy protection—one *Spruance* destroyer and nine frigates are the usual convoy escort force. Underway Replenishment Groups (URG) are guarded by three frigates and a guided missile destroyer (the new *Arleigh Burke* is slated to perform this role).

An underway replenishment group usually consists of three types of ships: oilers, ammunition ships, and stores ships. Oilers are tankers that carry ship and aviation fuels. Some of the AOs—fast combat support ships and underway replacement oilers—have been lengthened to carry other stores. Ammunition ships (AEs) haul reloads of guided missiles in containers that can be directly transferred from ship to ship. These AEs are nervously named after volcanoes. The stores ships (AFs and AFSs) carry food, water, and spare parts. Some sections of the store ships are refrigerated.

One or two AOs, an AE and an AF or AFS

Fleet oiler *Kalamazoo* shuttles from port to battle group.

Opposite: Inchon, an amphibious assault ship.

make up a typical underway replenishment group. It cycles back and forth from port to station. Sometimes the URG ships deliver their loads directly to the battle group. Usually, however, they transfer their load to a multi-product ship and then head back to base to load up again.

One or two multi-product ships travel with the battle group. The giant *Sacramento* class support ship is built to keep up with the fast carriers. The AOE (fast combat support ship) can make twenty-six knots and is armed with short-ranged missiles and guns. The smaller replenishment oilers (AORs) are somewhat slower. Built as an alternative to the expensive AOE, the AOR can still carry enough for two refuelings of a conventional aircraft carrier and its escorts. Nuclear-powered carriers need not be refueled, of course. In fact, they carry extra fuel for their escorts, as well as missile reloads and other supplies for the rest of the battle group.

Some of the replenishment ships are manned by the civilian crews of the Military Sealift Command. The Navy is responsible for all U.S. military equipment shipped overseas, but most of it is shuttled by civilians, using chartered merchant ships. In addition, MSC crews man freighters, tankers, and replenishment ships. Such ships are considered active Navy ships and are given the prefix "T" (for example, an MSC-manned ammunition ship of the Naval Fleet Auxiliary Force is designated T-AE).

The MSC crews may be civil servants, but they are not post office workers. They know what they're doing. A great many of the MSC hands are ex-Navy men. Underway replenishment is tricky business. Even in these days of automated systems, it takes a lot of know-how to pull it off safely. A lot of old-fashioned seamanship sails with the ships of the underway replenishment groups.

Underway replenishment is one of the most exciting sights on the ocean, especially at night. The oiler, surprisingly large, moves up slowly through the task group. It takes up station starboard of the black bulk of the aircraft carrier. Because of the restricted vision from the bridge, the flattop is the only ship the oiler approaches. All other ships must come to it.

Flashing lines shoot from the tanker. The crew on board the receiving ship catch the shot-line and rig a network of cables between the two ships. There are a variety of ways to get the 230-foot, 6″ fuel line from ship to ship. In the close-in method, ships steam about sixty feet apart. That's a dangerous distance, and doesn't allow the use of anti-aircraft guns. The span wire method gives a little more breathing room—the ships steam about 150 feet apart—and since the hose is carried higher over the waves, it's the method most frequently used in rough seas.

Most modern ships use a probe—or the older Robb coupling—at the end of the fuel line. Both methods are faster than the old "pigtail," which is simply a soft rubber hose shoved into the fuel tank and lashed into place. Most ships take fuel in more than one station, and there is often a spirited competition to see which one can get rigged and pumping first.

Even with the most modern methods, it takes an awfully long time to refuel at sea. Ships are particularly vulnerable during such an operation, which is why most refueling is done at night, with ships often serviced two at a time. It's the receiving ship's responsibility to keep station with the oiler. Mistakes happen.

Cargo is sometimes transferred in a similar manner, using lines and winches. The Navy has a completely mechanized system called FAST, or Fast Automatic Shuttle Transfer. FAST was designed to transfer missiles from the UNREP (underwing replacement) ship's cargo hold directly to the magazine of another ship. The system is also used for the movement of conventional cargo.

A great deal of freight also moves through the air, via vertical replenishment. The Navy's

VERTREP workhorse is the UH-46 Sea Knight. The choppers from the replenishment vessel flit from ship to ship like bees in a flower field, bringing spare parts, mail, cargo, and even people. Usually, the helicopter doesn't land. It hovers over the receiving ship's flight deck, while a crew unhitches the load slung in nets underneath. VERTREP is fast and efficient, but will never replace UNREP for transfer of bulk products.

The expansion to fifteen carrier battle groups will stretch the replenishment forces pretty thin. And the Navy pays the price for American presence around the globe with supply lines that often stretch thousands of miles in peacetime, and would most likely stretch even farther in war. A modern war at sea would consume supply at a ravenous rate as ships steam faster, stay longer, and fight day and night.

The Navy has recently come under criticism for its lack of war supply. A congressional study contended that the fleet could not participate in contemporary combat for a month, even a couple of weeks, before it ran out of missiles. Even if the supplies were handy, the far-flung bases are less than secure. And even if the bases escape attack, the fragile underway replenishment groups are tempting targets. Any way you look at it, supply could prove to be the fleet's Achilles' heel in the next war.

The Navy is getting a head start on supply by pre-positioning ships packed with equipment in hard-to-reach places. That's why the heavy stuff of a Marine Amphibious Brigade is bobbing on four ships in the Indian Ocean off Diego Garcia.

The Marine Corps muscle rests in three Marine Amphibious Forces. An MAF consists of a reinforced Marine infantry division and a Marine air wing. With about fifty thousand men, the MAF is the Marine's largest self-contained landing force. There is an MAF on each coast and a third scattered through the Pacific.

But the Navy has only about sixty amphibious ships, enough to transport one MAF at best. About 10 percent of that MAF is permanently embarked, in the form of a Marine Amphibious Unit. There are two MAUs constantly afloat, one in the Mediterranean with the Sixth Fleet, and one with the Seventh Fleet in the western Pacific. These groups of about twenty-five hundred men, along with some light armor and air elements, are used as peacekeepers and a quick reaction force.

The MAU sails in an Amphibious Ready Group, a Navy unit consisting of about half a dozen small landing craft, a couple of ships to carry them in and a helicopter carrier. Several MAUs combine to form a Marine Amphibious Brigade (MAB). Because of sealift restrictions, logistics, and the necessity of tactical surprise, the MAB, with some elements of a Marine Air Wing, is the most likely candidate to attempt opposed landings in combat.

This is not enough force to open up a second front, of course, but that's not the Marines' job. They're used as shock troops to open up a beachhead, or to move quickly to seize territory and wait for reinforcements. The bulk of the manpower will come later, when the Army arrives. The Marines do the dirty work, then move on.

The Marines are the ultimate rapid deployment force, at least on paper. They are a mobile, well-trained, integrated combined-arms team, ready, willing, and able to tackle the toughest jobs. The Marines say men, not machines, make the difference in combat. The story is, if it doesn't leak oil, shed parts, self-destruct, or smoke, it doesn't belong in the Marine Corps.

Sometimes they *do* get new equipment, whether they want it or not. The Marines saw the future in V/STOL (vertical/short take-off and landing); the Navy saw a threat to their carriers. The Marines wanted the Harrier; the Navy wanted them to buy the Hornet instead, to keep the costs down on the F-18 program and keep the lid on a technology that competes with the conventional carrier aircraft the Navy has staked *its* future on. The Marines went to the mat to get the AV-8B, but they wound up buying the F/A-18 as well.

Underway replenishment, Soviet style.

Both new planes, as well as the Marines' A-6 and EA-6, are designed to operate from both land and sea, even though the USMC has no ships of its own. Marine squadrons regularly fill in for Navy units on conventional carriers. The AV-8B is a different story. The Navy is building a brand new ship just to take the Harrier II to sea.

LHD-1 is the first of four new sea control ships built the way the Marines want them. *Wasp* and her three sister ships will carry twenty AV-8Bs and a half-dozen new SH-60B Sea Hawk helicopters. The design is based on the *Tarawa* class helicopter

A rare photo of both Navy amphibious command ships — *Blue Ridge* and *Mount Whitney* — together off Norfolk, Virginia. The ships were built for use by Marine assault force commanders but were commandeered by the Navy.

Underway replenishment in the Pacific: *New Jersey* (BB-62), *Kansas City* (AOR-3), and *Buchanan* (DDG-14).

carriers, with a larger well deck and a hundred-foot ski jump on the bow. The ski jump was invented by the British and tested in the Falklands. It allows the jump-jets to carry heavier loads by giving them a headstart in the air.

The Navy has toyed with the idea of V/STOL carriers for years. Back in 1973, as the Harriers were introduced in Marine Corps service, tests were conducted on the assault carrier *Guam*. Eight years later, further tests on the *Tarawa* class *Nassau* confirmed the V/STOL carrier concept. And with three new supercarriers authorized, the Navy could at last loosen up and allow a Harrier carrier to be built.

Although technically an amphibious assault ship, *Wasp* is more than just another "gator freighter." The Harriers can operate in conjunction with the Sea Hawk helicopters to protect the rest of the amphibious force, especially close to the shore. At sea, the AV-8Bs provide an always-welcome addition to the battle group air defense grid. They are particularly good at low-altitude and fast surface threats in the middle defense zone, where protection is sometimes lacking. And after the landing, when the big carriers have steamed away, *Wasp* and her aircraft can provide close air support and air cover for the invasion forces until an airstrip can be seized or built. In addition, with the helicopters on board connected to the LAMPS ASW system, the ship can provide some of its own antisubmarine support, something the amphibious forces have always had to depend upon other ships for.

Wasp and her successors will carry up to three Landing Craft Air Cushions (LCAC), a new type of landing craft that promises the biggest revolution in amphibious assault tactics since the helicopter. In fact, the LCAC resembles an aircraft in many ways. Riding on a cushion of air, the LCAC is pushed along by huge propellers on the bow, much like an airboat in the Everglades.

Up to a point, the LCAC is truly amphibious. It can negotiate swamps, marshes, mud, wet sand, and a lot of other terrain types that are neither earth nor water. Air cushion technology has opened up more than two-thirds of the world's beaches as possible landing sites, as opposed to the 17 percent that can be reached by other types of landing craft. It is also very fast—fifty knots, tops—with a two-hundred-mile radius of action. The LCAC's speed, range, and landing site versatility combine to put surprise and maneuver back into amphibious warfare.

It's taken two decades for LCACs to get to the fleet. The Soviet Navy has had them for years. Theirs aren't as good as ours, maybe, but they're *there*. The Navy plans to buy about half a dozen a year for the next ten years.

But there are drawbacks. LCACs are expensive—at least $10 million apiece. Both noisy and fragile, LCACs are also big, taking up a lot of room in the few ships large enough to carry them. A lot of that size is due to the large power plants that enable them to do what they do. LCACs are not that big inside. Although they can carry sixty tons, there's only enough room on deck for one main battle tank.

For those reasons, there aren't going to be enough LCACs to go around. The Navy could come up with a way to integrate them with older landing craft, but the prospect of integrating long-range, high-speed LCACs with short-range, low-speed traditional landing craft presents major tactical problems. More than likely, the limited numbers of LCACs will be grouped together in a special force and used for pre-invasion raids or as a first-wave assault leader.

Most of the Marines will come ashore in the older LCMs and LCUs. The "Mike Boat" is the traditional landing craft, only slightly changed from the ones in which John Wayne hit the beach in countless World War II movies. The LCU is larger, capable of ferrying three M-60 main battle tanks ashore. There are several sub-types of both landing craft, but all share the same design. The boat is beached, the armored bow ramp slams open, and assorted gyrenes, grunts, jar-heads and anchor-clankers come boiling ashore like a bunch of maniacs.

Some of the Marines will come directly on shore in amphibious tractors. The problems involved in building a truly amphibious infantry fighting vehicle have yet to be resolved. The Corps' thirty-knot LVA program was canceled in 1979 as too complex and expensive. A new program, the LVT (X) has run into delays. In any case, its eight-knot water speed won't offer much improvement in that respect. The Marines have decided to rebuild their ageless LVTPs and run them until something better comes along.

The Marines have nearly a thousand vehicles of the LVT-7 series. All share the same deficiencies. They can neither dish it out nor take it. Armed with only a machine gun, the LVTP is thin-skinned and vulnerable to hostile fire. Big and boxy, it presents quite a target.

As a landing craft, the "Superhog" also has problems. Although it boasts an advertised range of fifty-five miles in the water, the way the LVTP is used in combat severely restricts the distance it can travel to the beach. The Marines make the approach to the beach buttoned up. The noise, smoke, heat, and fumes inside the vehicle make it impossible for even the hardiest leatherneck to stand a cruise that lasts more than half an hour (although it does make them eager to get out!). At a maximum speed of eight knots, a thirty-minute ride means the LVTPs must be launched about three miles from the beach. Even if the amtracs are spewed from a moving ship—an operation that presents its own problems—the fleet is brought dangerously close to enemy defenses.

Usually, the fleet forms up for a landing about twenty-five miles offshore, over the horizon. The enemy knows something's up; friendly aircraft have swept the skies, reconnaissance planes drone overhead, and minesweepers are constantly sweeping the coast. It's unavoidable—landings can only take place in conditions of absolute air, sea, and

Spiegel Grove, a landing ship dock, off Hampton Roads, Virginia. An LTU assault craft returns to the ship's well deck.

subsurface superiority. Besides, in an era of spy satellites, it's almost impossible to hide something as big as an invasion fleet.

But even if strategic surprise is impossible, *tactical* surprise is not. The enemy may know an amphibious assault is coming, but he doesn't know where. In theory, the fleet can steam nearly five hundred miles a day, although this may be a bit optimistic. ("The true speed of the twenty-knot amphibious force," says one naval observer, "is sixteen knots.") In any case, out of hundreds of miles of coastline, the defender is never quite sure which two or three miles the Marines will choose for a beachhead. The mobility of LCACs makes amphibious surprise attacks possible. But even with ordinary landing craft, it's possible to achieve some level of surprise, using diversionary raids, electronic discipline, night landings, and helicopter encirclement.

A full MAF landing will use more than two hundred landing craft. An assault by an MAB will use a fraction of that, ferried to the line of departure by fifteen or twenty amphibious warfare ships. Helicopter carriers can transport landing craft underneath the flight deck, but the bulk of the assault boats will be carried by LSDs and LPDs (which also carry personnel).

The LVTPs will go in first. If surprise is lost, or

not deemed as important as softening up the defenses, the beach will be pounded with naval gunfire and air strikes. Minesweepers will have cleared lanes leading to the beachhead. (The LCAC makes a good minesweeper because of its low displacement and rubber "hull.") The wave-guide commander will be in one of the two primary control ships that mark the boundaries of the landing zone.

The LVTPs go in line-abreast, carrying assault troops and combat engineers. More light infantry move in on the second wave. They have no heavy weapons. If their mission is a success, the tanks and artillery will arrive on LCUs on the third and fourth waves. The whole thing takes less than ten minutes.

Or at least, that's the plan. But amphibious landings are tricky. There is no such thing as a "classic" amphibious assault. There are too many variables; something always goes wrong. The

Coast Guard *Hamilton* class cutter *Sherman,* en route to Alaska for ten-week law enforcement patrol. Although thought of only as life-saving vessels, the high-endurance cutters are equipped for combat missions. *Photo by Hans Halberstadt.*

Marines know this. To paraphrase the common wisdom, the things that make Marines difficult to deal with in peacetime make them invaluable in wartime. They improvise, they take their lumps, and if there's a way it can be done, they'll do it.

Like the Marines, the Coast Guard is controlled in wartime by the Navy. But in peacetime, the Coast Guard is under the orders of a civilian agency, the Department of Transportation. The two masters give the Coast Guard a dual person-

ality as it performs its usual tasks in peacetime while preparing for war.

Combat is nothing new to the Coast Guard. Since its formation nearly two hundred years ago, Coast Guard personnel have taken part in nearly

F-5 and A-4 "adversary" aircraft from Top Gun, the Navy Fighter Weapons School at NAS Miramar, California.

every war the U.S. has fought. The service conducted ASW patrols in both world wars, search and rescue in Korea, and Market Time warfare (coastal patrol) in Vietnam. Most recently, Coast Guard ships took over protection of Grenada after the Navy invasion fleet steamed away.

The Coast Guard has seen a lot of wartime action, but there is perhaps more danger in carrying out its peacetime patrols. At least in war, one knows who the enemy is. Imagine what a young guardsman must go through, calling a boat to heave to in the middle of the night, not knowing if the people on board are panic-stricken vacationers or heavily armed drug runners. In fact, the Coast Guard has seen more real action lately than the Navy has. The crackdown on drug runners has produced some tense moments on the high seas, especially in the Caribbean.

The Coast Guard is charged with a number of other, less dangerous missions. In addition to their well known role in search and rescue, the Guard is also responsible for safety inspections of ships, ports and bridges, and the maintenance of navigational aids. One aspect of the Coast Guard's mission that doesn't get much publicity is the resupply of American military installations near the North Pole and civilian installations in Antarctica. The Coast Guard uses five icebreakers for the lonely voyages to the top and bottom of the world.

The Coast Guard fleet would be the envy of many navies. Among its larger vessels are a dozen *Hamilton* class high endurance cutters. Armed with a 5″ gun, torpedo tubes, and full helicopter facilities, the *Hamilton*s are powerful enough to take their place, in wartime, with the carrier battle group or as a convoy escort. The same role is planned for the new *Bear* class cutters, which carry a 3″ gun and ASW systems (and may even get Phalanx and Harpoon later on). Critics say the *Bear* is too slow and lacks range, but the Coast Guard is happy to get the new ships. They've also got their eye on the Navy's *Oliver Hazard Perry* class frigates. The Navy seems to want to get rid of them. If that's the case, the Coast Guard would love to have them.

The Naval Reserve has already gotten some *Perry*s, the first new equipment they've received in years. For a long time, the regular Navy wasn't getting many new ships, so the Reserve had it even rougher. Now, they're getting brand new equipment, including the F/A-18. A Reserve outfit in California was among the first to receive the Hornet. The Navy hopes to be able to continue the trend.

Like the Air Force and Army reserves, the Naval Reserve is far from being the group of "weekend warriors" often pictured in the press. Much of the nation's combat skill is vested in the reserves. In many exercises, they come out ahead of their active duty counterparts. There's no substitute for experience, and the Reserves train enough to be ready should they be called up.

In particular, the Naval Air Reserve is a valuable national asset. There are two Reserve carrier air wings, CVWR 20 on the East Coast, and CVWR 30 on the West Coast. Although, in general, they fly hand-me-downs from the fleet, the Reserves make a good showing in fleet exercises. The Reserve air wings sometimes deploy to a carrier for practice workups. There's even been talk about carrying a composite Reserve squadron aboard for an entire cruise, although it would be tough for the pilots, many of whom fly for commercial airlines, to get away for any length of time, short of a national emergency.

The USN has a number of relatively small, but interesting organizations that also bear mention, as long as we're on the subject of *other* U.S. navies.

The SeaBees are the Navy's master builders on shore. The original SeaBees were a group of civilian construction workers who volunteered during World War II. They were organized into construction battalions (hence the name). In the Pacific, the SeaBees built airstrips and port facilities.

Today, they play a major role in screening foreign contractors building American facilities abroad. They also perform some minor construction themselves, for American embassies and bases around the world.

The SEALS are the Navy's commandos. The name stands for Sea-Air-Land teams, and that's exactly what they are. Trained in a variety of war skills, they can parachute in, drop from helicopters, row in silently on rafts from a submarine offshore, or swim in using scuba gear. A big part of their job is scouting ahead of an amphibious invasion, perhaps even planting electronic beacons to guide aircraft and direct shore bombardment. But they won't clear obstacles on the beach; that's the job of the UDT (Underwater Demolition Teams). The SEALS were the first Americans on shore during the Grenada invasion.

The Blue Angels are the Navy's flight demonstration team. There are a great many aerobatic teams in the world, but the Blues are something special. If they are not the best, they are certainly the best known. From their base at NAS Pensacola, Florida, the Blue Angels have traveled around the world. Their blue and gold jets are a familiar sight to most aviation enthusiasts. The Blues' performances will take on a new dimension soon when they trade in their A-4s for brand new Hornets.

If a tour with the Blue Angels looks good on a naval officer's record, it's nothing compared with a degree from the Naval Academy. The academy at Annapolis, Maryland, takes only the best; high school and prep school candidates must be nominated by their congressmen before they'll even be considered (although a few Navy enlisted men are also admitted each year). The Naval Academy is a good school, academically, but what is really taught is an attitude. Midshipmen leave as boomer ensigns, complete with a gold ring, a feeling of invincibility, and a set of preconceptions that may or may not prove true in the real world. We'll discuss some of those in the next chapter.

Chapter Seven

Seapower and the State

All hail Sergei Georgiyevich Gorshkov, Admiral of the Fleet of the Soviet Union, Naval Thinker, Consummate Politician, Civil Servant, and First Class Production Hero!

Gorshkov does not look like the Governor of the Great Ocean. He's retired now; after all, he was born in 1910, the year of the first flight of an aircraft from the deck of a ship. And without his glasses, Gorshkov would resemble Rodney Dangerfield, were it not for that cold fish stare common to big-time Soviet leaders.

But make no mistake, Gorshkov is still a real heavyweight. He has single handedly led the Soviet Navy out onto the Great Ocean, as surely as if he'd grabbed his boats by the bow and waded out into the blue water himself. And he's done it pretty much alone, through bluffs, intimidation, skillful political maneuvering, and unwavering dedication. He is very much the father of the modern Soviet Navy, and that fleet resembles the man in all respects: ambitious, innovative, and aggressive, stumbling at times, but always ready for the next step.

Gorshkov was not only commander-in-chief of the Soviet Navy, he also served as Deputy Minister

Destroyer *Preble* caught between A-6 fuel tanks. *Photo by Michael Skinner.*

of Defense and a full member of the Communist Party's Central Committee. That made him equivalent to both the civilian Secretary of the Navy and the uniformed Chief of Naval Operations. Gorshkov could dream things up and then make sure they came true. Of course, that enormous power could have led to unchecked failures, of which he had plenty, trying to move too fast too soon. But Gorshkov's administrative muscle, coupled with his experience on the job—he'd been running the Navy since 1956—and not a little help from his unsung predecessor, allowed him to translate his vision of a Russian fleet fit for the Great Ocean into steel and steam.

What, then, is Admiral Gorshkov's ultimate goal for his Navy? That is hard to figure. You can't really go by what he says. His book, *Seapower and the State,* is remarkable only for its ability to mean different things to each reader. Even his clear statements are not often reliable. In 1967 he wrote that the aircraft carrier was finished; since then, the Soviets have built half a dozen.

On the other hand, one can argue—as Gorshkov has no doubt done before the politburo—that the Soviet carriers and his other shiny new ships are built to hunt down American ballistic missile submarines and keep the USN off the backs of the

Soviet *Kiev* class guided missile VSTOL aircraft carrier *Kiev*. The Soviet Navy has always shown a willingness to go its own way in warship design.

Red Army, two goals very much in line with Kremlin thinking. But Gorshkov seems to have something bigger on his mind—a fleet that can challenge the mighty USN on the Great Ocean.

For years now, the prying eyes of American spy satellites have been staring at Nikolayev Chernomorskij on the Black Sea. There, in Shipyard 444, the Soviet Union has built its first real aircraft carrier.

Estimated to weigh 65,000 tons and measure 1,000 feet, the ship is still not quite as large as the newer American behemoths. But it's a big step up from the relatively dinky helicopter cruisers and antisubmarine carriers that have characterized the first steps of the Bear into the deeper waters of carrier aviation. (Ironically, the Soviet Union's first real aircraft carrier may be classified as an "aviation battleship" to permit passage through the Straits of Turkey, prohibited to carriers by treaty.)

Unfortunately, despite what you have read, that is all we really know about Black-Com-2, the U.S. Navy's sinister code name for the new carrier. (Actually, the proper designation is Bal-Com-2,

for the second surface combatant building in the Baltic. But the other name sounds so much more menacing that no one uses the correct one anymore.) Satellites cannot peek into people's heads. The Russians aren't talking about their new carrier, but everyone else is. This is what they're saying:

The new carrier is almost certainly nuclear powered, a trend begun with the *Kirov* battle cruiser. It may also borrow some of *Kirov*'s weapons systems, including the vertical launch tubes, for its *Kiev*-like bow, although some reports suggest the new ship will have a through-deck similar to American carriers, with the hatches of the vertical launch tubes mounted flush on the forward flight deck.

Most estimates say the new carrier will embark around seventy-five aircraft, although reports differ on the type. The new Helix naval helicopters are sure bets, and navalized versions of the swing-wing Su-24 Fencer strike aircraft and MiG-27 Flogger fighter-bomber are often mentioned. But *Jane's* says the emphasis will be on "fixed-wing interceptor-attack aircraft," even though no likely candidates for this role are yet apparent. Given the Soviet penchant for electronic combat and their need for over-the-horizon targeting, other types of support aircraft are likely to be carried, although, again, there is no evidence of any such aircraft being tested.

No one even knows the true name of the new carrier. *Leonid Brezhnev* came and went (although the name was bandied about for the second *Kirov* before that ship was known to be christened *Frunze*). The new carrier was also called *Sovetskiy Soyuz* (Soviet Union), but now the press seems to have settled on *Kremlin* as the best guess.

One thing *is* certain. Although Black-Com-2 has been launched, it will be a long time before it poses a real blue water, blue sky threat to the USN. Even if it were to set sail tomorrow with all the aircraft on board, it would still take years before the carrier could become operational. For the Soviets, *Kremlin* is not just another ship. It's another world.

Carrier ops is a folk art. The U.S. Navy, which is built around the supercarrier, has a cadre of officers and men who have learned the lessons of the flight deck the hard way. The knowledge is passed from sailor to sailor. But even though American carrier crews are recognized as the best in the world at what they do, mistakes still happen. Given the generally poorer skill level of Soviet sailors, their new carrier will have to weather a series of long and difficult shakedown cruises before reaching smooth sailing.

The Soviet Union is preparing as best it can. Russian ships shadowing American task forces have been very interested in launches and recoveries as of late. And for years, Soviet pilots have reportedly been practicing on a full-scale outline of the carrier's flight deck sketched out on concrete at Saki naval air base off the Black Sea. The Soviets are also working on catapults and arresting gear there, although, even at this late date, some experts believe the ship will use a ski jump in place of steam catapults. All the newest Russian aircraft, including the Su-27 Flanker, the MiG-29 Fulcrum fighters, and the Su-25 Frogfoot ground attack aircraft have rolled off the ski jumps at Saki, although it's difficult to say if this is just pure research or if the aircraft are actually destined to sail on the new carrier.

The U.S. Navy is flattered by the attention, but they have mixed feelings about Black-Com-2. The idea of Soviet attack carriers prowling the Great Ocean—and there are reports that as many as seven more *Kremlins* will be constructed—does not sit well with American naval planners. Even if only one is completed, and the Russians suffer the problems expected learning the fine art of flight ops, *Kremlin* will usher in a new era of warfare on the Great Ocean. U.S. naval aviators will no longer be alone in the sky over the blue water. The spectre of supercarrier battles in mid-ocean will demand a significant change in American maritime strategy.

On the other hand, the first reports of a new Soviet carrier building couldn't have come at better time for the U.S. Navy. The news from Shipyard 444 arrived just as the Navy was trying to push three new supercarriers through Congress. The *Kremlin* served the lobbyists well, both as a threat and proof that the carrier was *not* just an American anachronism.

Aircraft carriers have an impact greater than any other weapon system. They also have a greater number of advocates—and detractors.

The modern nuclear supercarrier is no doubt a powerful military asset, able to sail for thirteen years without refueling, carrying an armada of versatile tactical aircraft that can reach targets just about anywhere on the globe. A carrier battle group can theoretically control six hundred miles of ocean, above, beneath, and on the surface. They are movable, and cannot be overrun, which is not true with land bases—of the dozens of air bases built by the U.S. on the Asian mainland *not one* remains available to American forces today.

On the other hand, aircraft carriers are tremendously expensive. A conservative estimate of the cost of a *Nimitz* class supercarrier is around $3 billion. That's a pretty big chunk in itself, but with its air wing, submarine, and surface escort, the modern carrier battle group costs at least 17 billion not even counting operating costs. That's the biggest price tag in the entire defense budget, more than a hundred B-1 bombers, or seventy-five MX missiles. Carriers are also a huge drain on the Navy's dwindling manpower, especially in the critical nuclear engineering field.

And worse, they can be sunk. The question of the extent of the carrier's vulnerability to modern cruise missiles is still being debated. Both sides point to the Falklands war to support their arguments, but the fact is the war in the Malvinas was too limited in scope to garner any hard evidence. Still, it is hard to ignore the image of sixteen British ships damaged or sunk, burning in the freezing waters at the bottom of the world.

The truth is probably somewhere between the two poles. The carrier is much more difficult to bag than the critics would have us believe. Defense analyst Jim Dunnigan figures that less than 3 percent of the Soviet cruise missiles fired at Western task forces would get through. He bases the estimate on World War II Kamikaze warfare—if anything, the suicide planes were more accurately guided than today's weapons—and American versus Russian technology. (Dunnigan says Western cruise missiles could be as much as ten times more accurate than Soviet weapons.)

There *will* be hits—up to a dozen if the Soviets manage to get off the estimated four hundred cruise missiles potentially aimed at each carrier group. The supercarriers are built to take up to four hits and keep functioning, although the small boys in the task force could be sunk or disabled after just one hit. However, it's doubtful the USN would put its precious carriers in a position in which they would suffer the onslaught of a complete Soviet attack, or that the Russians would be able to get off a fraction of that number of missiles in the face of an American counterattack.

But some Navy skippers are more than a little concerned about Navy Secretary John Lehman's talk about sailing up the Kola Peninsula to keep Soviet subs bottled up at their bases in the Arctic Sea. As a civilian, Lehman has no direct control over American naval operations, and perhaps this is a good thing. Although Lehman argues that land-based air power would help the battle groups pull it off (contradicting his arguments that land-based air power is obsolete and carrier battle groups can protect themselves independently), most naval experts consider an attack against four hundred Soviet ships, subs, and countless aircraft at the main-force Soviet bases in the early stages of a conventional war a suicide mission. As for Lehman, an A-6 bombardier-navigator in the Naval Reserve, should he somehow point a carrier towards the Barents Sea in wartime, he is likely to find himself, helmet in hand, alone on deck with just a single pilotless Intruder running up on the catapult.

Even without sailing into the Bear's mouth, carriers are not likely to survive long in a nuclear war. We said before that weapons are useless in peacetime and priceless in war, but the supercarriers are the exception. They are an invaluable asset for force projection in peace and tactical support in limited war, but in an all-out global nuclear conflict most are likely to be eliminated at their bases in the first wave.

For all the Navy's talk about the carrier's mobility and global range, the fact is that aircraft carriers spend most of their time in port or traveling to and from station. This is more of a support problem than any fault of the carriers' design, but it is still a big headache for Navy planners.

At any given time, about one-third of the Navy's carriers will be in port, refitting for the next voyage. One of the carriers will be undergoing a major overhaul called the Service Life Extension Program, or SLEP. A carrier put to SLEP will be out for a long time, perhaps two years or more. The program gives the Navy more carriers in the long run, but puts pressure on an already tight deployment schedule. Another third of the USN carrier force is out of action while steaming to station or returning to port after being relieved. The Navy likes to keep four carriers on the Great Ocean and another in reserve, ready to sail.

The recent commitment to keep a naval presence on station in the Indian Ocean has stretched the Navy thin at a time when many older ships are due for retirement or are undergoing extensive refit. The USN, as the saying goes, has become "a one-and-a-half ocean navy with a three-ocean commitment." That's why they need the new carriers.

The new American supercarriers will be built, but the issue was touch and go for a while. Many

congressmen fought desperately for an alternative to the huge, expensive, and increasingly vulnerable nuclear-powered supercarrier. And during the reign of Elmo Zumwalt—the first surface Navy man to become chief of naval operations after a long line of carrier admirals—critics of the supercarriers found an ally.

Zumwalt thought the USN's preoccupation with the war in Southeast Asia—essentially a carrier show, from the Navy's standpoint—had led to a decline in surface warfare capability. Numbers were what was needed in NATO. Zumwalt's "Project 60" called for a "high-low" mix of ships that would supplement the Navy's few and expensive modern warships with a large number of relatively cheap ones.

Several proposals were put forth, ranging from a conventionally powered carrier almost as large as the *John F. Kennedy* class to a much smaller sea control ship. Many recommended the U.S. follow the Soviets and the British in building a V/STOL carrier. Some even suggested America had enough carriers and no further building was necessary.

With Zumwalt's retirement in 1974, the carrier Navy counterattacked viciously. Defense is never cheap, they said, but the smaller carriers were no bargain. Nuclear carriers carry nearly twice the aviation fuel of a conventionally powered carrier, and 50 percent more ammunition. A smaller carrier, such as the Navy's Design Study 45—a 44,000-ton sea control ship with less than half the aircraft of a *Nimitz* class carrier and very little battle damage protection—would still cost about two-thirds the price of a new supercarrier.

Not only was the CVLX-45 less than cost-effective, said the Navy, it was not a viable weapons system. To carry the interceptors, airborne warning aircraft, subchasers, and electronic warfare platforms needed to survive in modern sea warfare, CVLX-45 would have to give up its attack squadrons, its offensive punch. As for the carrier concept being obsolete, the Navy said, the aircraft carrier will be obsolete only when aircraft are obsolete.

So the Navy will get its three new supercarriers. *Theodore Roosevelt* is undergoing trials, while work is well under way on both *Abraham Lincoln*

Enterprise, with its rebuilt island, returns to port. Controversy follows the carriers wherever they sail.

and *George Washington* in Newport News. And it looks like the Soviet Union will get its new carrier too, but the debate is far from over.

There's a new storm brewing on the horizon for the supercarrier. This time, the criticism comes not from outsiders, but from the heart of the Navy itself. And the debate isn't about the carriers as such—to these naval officers, the utility of the modern supercarrier is beyond question—but with the way they are used.

Weapons and strategy are interlocked. New technology affects strategy, certainly, just as strategy plays a major part in the kinds of weapons that are developed. The Navy's crush on the aircraft carrier is a perfect example of this. Is current naval strategy built around the supercarrier, or is the supercarrier built to carry out current naval strategy? It is a moot point. Barring catastrophe or loss in combat, the USN's new carriers will be sailing at least until today's Annapolis graduates take over the helm.

Naval planning takes years to develop. Today's world can change in the flash of an explosion. It may already be ahead of current American naval thinking. The Navy prides itself on being the first, and often only, U.S. service on the scene at hotspots around the globe. But the days of presidents

dispatching an aircraft carrier as if it were an angry letter to the editor may soon be over. A growing number of voices in the Navy's professional press say that if the carriers continue to park off the scene of world crisis spots they are headed for trouble.

The Navy has a philosophy called "modified local operations," or ModLocs for short. At the first sign of trouble, the carrier battle group is dispatched to the scene, where it sails around in circles. The area described by the circle is a ModLoc, an imaginary tract drawn on the water that defines the operating perimeter of a carrier battle group. Perhaps the most famous ModLoc is Yankee Station, off the North Vietnamese coast. There are others: Gonzo Station is off Oman in the north Arabian Sea; Bagel Station is in the Eastern Med, off Israel. Other ModLocs include Kermit Station, Parrot Station, and dozens of other points familiar to most carrier sailors.

There are good things about ModLocs. They simplify the huge logistics problems that follow carrier battle groups around the globe. Since rapid communications are imperative in the sensitive areas bordering most ModLocs, they help make sure the carriers don't wander off where they can't be reached rapidly. And, again, since the carriers are operating where a false move could have international repercussions, ModLocs keep the task force grouped where the commander can keep a close eye on every part.

There are bad things about ModLocs, as well. With their familiar supply lines, they don't help train our sailors in the improvisation of logistics that will be a vital part of any war. Since everyone knows where the carrier battle group is, there's no sense in maintaining electronic silence, another crucial wartime skill that needs constant practice.

But the most dangerous part of the ModLoc philosophy is that, in addition to not serving the purpose it's intended to, it leaves the precious carrier group open to attack. With today's long-range weapons and often irrational adversaries, a battle

group steaming off a hostile coast is not a threat, it's a target. The carriers and their escorts, tied in nets of political, logistical, and tactical restraints, are sitting ducks cutting circular grooves in the waters off the most dangerous parts of the world. And it won't be long before someone decides that the battle group, filling the air with radar beams, radio waves, sonar soundings, smoke, and noise, is too easy a shot to pass up.

The Navy is slowly beginning to realize this. In the eastern Med off Lebanon, it was not uncommon to see crews mounting fifty-caliber machine guns and Marines on guard with Stinger shoulder-

Bainbridge (CGN-25) and a *Knox* class frigate operate on Gonzo Station in the Indian Ocean.

launched missiles on the catwalks of American ships. The irony of men defending America's most technologically advanced warships with relatively primitive weapons could not have been lost on Navy brass.

As a modern version of gunboat diplomacy, the ModLoc concept is rapidly going out of date. Intimidation needs the threat of force behind it. The idea of offering an American supercarrier as hostage isn't going to solve anything. It worked

107

well for a while because it was expedient. It didn't really involve American troops in combat on foreign soil—the president's greatest worry—and it satisfied the modern American penchant for substituting technology for manpower.

But what if the bad guys aren't afraid of machines? What if the bad guys aren't afraid of anything? What if the floating diplomats have to fight to make their point?

Navy carriers on Yankee Station continuously pounded North Vietnam for years, but, in the end, it didn't make any difference (although, to be fair, nothing else the U.S. did in that war seemed to work either). More recently, two carriers off Lebanon sent a twenty-eight-plane Alfa Strike against three antiaircraft sites that had fired on F-14 reconnaissance planes. The Pentagon says the raid was "very successful" although detailed results were not released. And the Navy says the raid put a stop to further attacks on American recon aircraft. It *is* known that the U.S. lost two aircraft; one pilot was rescued, another was killed, and a third crewman—Lt. Robert Goodman—was at the center of an international incident when he was captured, and later released through the efforts of the Rev. Jesse Jackson.

No one really knows if an American fleet in the window has ever prevented a war, or helped cause one. The USN has intervened on more than two hundred occasions since World War II, but these days, with the troublemakers seeking to draw the U.S. into conflict, not keep it out, a carrier pacing off the world's hot spots is a dangerous temptation. Even an attempted suicide attack on the carriers could lead to serious trouble for everyone concerned. The Libyans have bought some fast Swedish powerboats that would be perfect for a Kamikaze run at an American carrier. (The carriers off Bagel Station were expecting a similar attack by private aircraft packed with explosives.)

Does this mean the Navy should give up its coveted role as America's peacetime policeman? Of course not. But the carriers' new critics say the Navy should change its tactics; come in silently, hit hard, and get out quick. Hanging around the ModLoc doesn't do anything except increase the carrier's vulnerability.

The Navy has worked hard to make the carriers viable. They have filled the flight decks with expensive, long-range interceptors to knock down bombers and long-range cruise missiles. They've built early warning radar planes to guard over the carriers and antisubmarine aircraft to keep watch underneath them.

It is an intricate, expensive, and imposing defense. It might work. But it is a *defense.* It is not the Navy way. The USN can argue that the best offense is a good defense, that the only way to sucker the Soviets into coming out to fight is to offer the carriers as bait. But the idea of the Navy leading with its jaw is disturbing to a lot of critics, not all of them out of uniform. As one authority puts it: "If you're going to be a duck in the shooting gallery, then you've got to design a very, very invulnerable duck."

The carriers have seen plenty of peacetime action, but never against the Soviet Union. Perhaps it's time to realize that the enemy doesn't always wear a red star and start building for the types of actions the carriers have actually been fighting since World War II—the projection of power on land. This is what the Marines have been saying all along, of course. But the Navy rarely listens to what the Marines have to say.

The critics claim that too much of the supercarrier's flight deck is taken up with defensive aircraft, and that too many of the Navy's ships are designed with only carrier air defense in mind. The great carrier battle groups *may* turn out to be as invulnerable as the Navy advertises, but they lack offensive punch.

Carrier supporters counter with this line: The Navy is not alone in this design philosophy. Even the mighty Soviet cruiser *Kirov* carries only twenty cruise missiles for offensive attack. The rest of its huge hull is filled with defensive antiair and antisubmarine weapons, systems and electronics. And after the Backfires are neutralized and the subs sunk on their way back from patrol, then the carriers become an unchallenged instrument for power projection. An Alfa Strike from a single aircraft carrier could deliver more than half a million pounds of bombs. And the planes will be back for another airstrike the next day, while the missiles would be lost forever.

There is a third possibility beyond the annihilation of either fleet. It could be that both sides, reluctant to expose their precious fleets unless they have a clear advantage, will circle one another endlessly on the Great Ocean, like boxers waiting for an opening that never comes. It could be that the next war at sea will resemble the first world war on land, a kind of trench warfare on the high seas in which no one gets to the carriers, but the carriers can't get to anyone else, either.

In the supercharged atmosphere surrounding the supercarriers, it's tough to get a reasonable dialogue started about the carriers' role now and into the next century. The supercarriers have taken on an importance even beyond their expense and importance in the Navy's order of battle. They have become floating icons. Zealots instinctively move to smite down blasphemy against the supercarrier and its floating and flying vassals. Carrier iconoclasts will hear nothing good about the obviously useful ships; they are devils and must be done away with without any thought of what could take their place.

Although the role of the carrier—or the attack submarine, or any other naval weapons system— is constantly being debated, the worth of the Navy itself is beyond question. There was a time, in the dawn of the atomic era, when analysts felt sea power, like so many other military endeavors, had been rendered superfluous by the bomb. Now it's recognized that just the opposite is true: the nation that controls the sea controls the world. And despite a growing threat from the Soviet fleet, the USN still rules the waves.

Above: Carriers have been described as sitting ducks. Here ordnance men install a fifty-caliber machine gun on the starboard island. *Photo by Michael Skinner.*

Below: "Wings over America." A pair of Black Lions from VF-213 overfly CV-66.

Perry class frigate, *Halyburton.*

Appendix I

U.S. Navy
Organization Chart

Department of the Navy

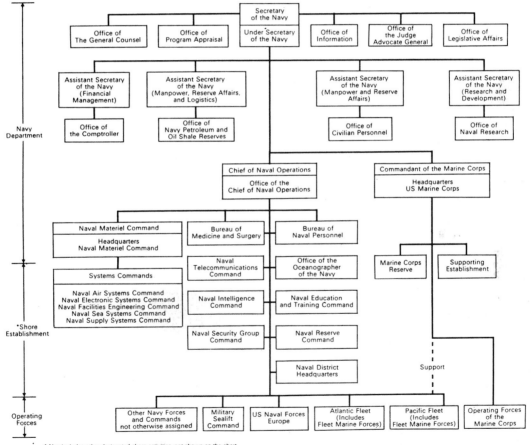

* Also includes other designated shore activities, not shown on the chart,
which are under the command or supervision of many of the organizations depicted.

Note: Chart is current as of 1985. Ongoing reorganization will result in changes during 1986.

Appendix II

U.S. Ranks and Ratings
A Comparison

While ranks are fairly comparative throughout the other services, the Navy has chosen, once again, to go its own way. This chart, reprinted with the kind permission of the U.S. Naval Institute from their invaluable *Bluejacket's Manual,* may help clear up some confusion. And explain, once and for all, the big difference between a captain in the Air Force and a captain in the Navy.

By the way, the USN has recently brought back the rank of Commodore. Formerly used merely as an honorific for any naval officer in command of a group of ships in wartime, the *rank* of Commodore has now been institutionalized, if only because it sounds so much more classy than Rear Admiral.

Guided Missile destroyer.

113

NAVY	MARINES	ARMY	AIR FORCE	
MASTER CHIEF P.O.	SGT. MAJOR / MASTER GUNNERY SGT.	SERGEANT MAJOR / COMMAND SERGEANT MAJOR	CHIEF MASTER SGT.	E-9
SENIOR CHIEF P.O.	1ST SGT. / MASTER SGT.	FIRST SERGEANT / MASTER SERGEANT	SENIOR MASTER SGT.	E-8
CHIEF P.O.	GUNNERY SGT.	SGT. 1ST CLASS	MASTER SGT.	E-7
P.O. 1ST CLASS	STAFF SGT.	STAFF SGT. / SPEC. 6	TECHNICAL SGT.	E-6
P.O. 2ND CLASS	SGT.	SGT. / SPEC. 5	STAFF SGT.	E-5
P.O. 3RD CLASS	CORPORAL	CORPORAL / SPEC. 4	SENIOR AIRMAN	E-4
SEAMAN	LANCE CORPORAL	PRIVATE 1ST CLASS	AIRMAN 1ST CLASS	E-3
SEAMAN APPRENTICE	PRIVATE 1ST CLASS	PRIVATE	AIRMAN	E-2
SEAMAN RECRUIT	PRIVATE	PRIVATE	BASIC AIRMAN	E-1

NAVY	MARINE CORPS	COAST GUARD	ARMY	AIR FORCE
W-2 CHIEF WARRANT OFFICER	GOLD SCARLET / W-1 WARRANT OFFICER — GOLD SCARLET / W-2 CHIEF WARRANT OFFICER	W-1 WARRANT OFFICER — W-2 CHIEF WARRANT OFFICER	SILVER BLACK / WO-1 WARRANT OFFICER — SILVER BLACK / CW-2 CHIEF WARRANT OFFICER	GOLD SKY BLUE / W-1 WARRANT OFFICER — GOLD SKY BLUE / W-2 CHIEF WARRANT OFFICER
W-3 CHIEF WARRANT OFFICER — W-4 CHIEF WARRANT OFFICER	SILVER SCARLET / W-3 CHIEF WARRANT OFFICER — SILVER SCARLET / W-4 CHIEF WARRANT OFFICER	W-3 CHIEF WARRANT OFFICER — W-4 CHIEF WARRANT OFFICER	SILVER BLACK / CW-3 CHIEF WARRANT OFFICER — SILVER BLACK / CW-4 CHIEF WARRANT OFFICER	SILVER SKY BLUE / W-3 CHIEF WARRANT OFFICER — SILVER SKY BLUE / W-4 CHIEF WARRANT OFFICER
ENSIGN	(GOLD) SECOND LIEUTENANT	ENSIGN	(GOLD) SECOND LIEUTENANT	(GOLD) SECOND LIEUTENANT
LIEUTENANT JUNIOR GRADE	(SILVER) FIRST LIEUTENANT	LIEUTENANT JUNIOR GRADE	(SILVER) FIRST LIEUTENANT	(SILVER) FIRST LIEUTENANT
LIEUTENANT	(SILVER) CAPTAIN	LIEUTENANT	(SILVER) CAPTAIN	(SILVER) CAPTAIN
LIEUTENANT COMMANDER	(GOLD) MAJOR	LIEUTENANT COMMANDER	(GOLD) MAJOR	(GOLD) MAJOR
COMMANDER	(SILVER) LIEUTENANT COLONEL	COMMANDER	(SILVER) LIEUTENANT COLONEL	(SILVER) LIEUTENANT COLONEL

NAVY	MARINE CORPS	COAST GUARD	ARMY	AIR FORCE
CAPTAIN	COLONEL	CAPTAIN	COLONEL	COLONEL
COMMODORE	BRIGADIER GENERAL	COMMODORE	BRIGADIER GENERAL	BRIGADIER GENERAL
REAR ADMIRAL	MAJOR GENERAL	REAR ADMIRAL	MAJOR GENERAL	MAJOR GENERAL
VICE ADMIRAL	LIEUTENANT GENERAL	VICE ADMIRAL	LIEUTENANT GENERAL	LIEUTENANT GENERAL
ADMIRAL	GENERAL	ADMIRAL	GENERAL	GENERAL
FLEET ADMIRAL	NONE	NONE	GENERAL OF THE ARMY	GENERAL OF THE AIR FORCE

From *The Bluejackets' Manual*, 20th ed., revised by Bill Bearden and Bill Wedertz. Copyright U.S. Naval Institute, Annapolis, Maryland.

Appendix III

U.S. Navy Organization and Deployment

American combat sailors belong to two navies. For training and major maintenance, it's convenient to organize ships of similar types into units called groups and squadrons. Generally, even-numbered units are based on the East Coast, and odd-numbered units on the West. This is a listing of major USN homeports, along with the types of ships and organizations based there.

I have taken the liberty of translating the unit designations into plain, non-acronymic English. The "correct" Navy title for a submarine group, for example, is "SubGru"; a destroyer squadron is actually a "DesRon." You get the idea. (My favorite is CruDesGru, which sounds like an industrial solvent but is actually a Cruiser/Destroyer Group.) I have also combined some different ship types together, such as CGNs with CGs and DDGs with DDs. This was done to save space, but in the squadrons and groups, different sub-types of ships are lumped together anyway. Also to save space, amphibious ships, minesweepers, and auxiliaries have been omitted.

Sailors belong to a different type of organization afloat. When deployed, ships are assigned to groups called Task Forces. These are often broken down into their component parts, called Task Groups, and identified by the initials "TG," a dash, and a series of numbers denoting, in order, the numbered fleet in operational command, the primary mission of the group, and, if there's more than one such unit in the fleet, a decimal followed by an identifying number. Thus, TG-60.2 is the second battle group in the Sixth Fleet Task Force (and can also be referred to as simply "Battle Force Bravo").

The whole thing is actually even *more* complicated than it sounds here. There are major organizational differences, for instance, between the chains of command in the Pacific and Atlantic fleets. And there's a similar schizophrenic chain of command for naval air units. But this list should give you a quick look at where the Navy's muscle is.

Atlantic Fleet

Second Fleet

HQ Norfolk, VA

Portland, ME	2 Destroyers
	2 Frigates
	Surface Squadron 2 (Naval Reserve Force)
	Destroyer Squadron 8

New London, CT	7 Attack Submarines
	Submarine Group 2
	Submarine Squadron 10
Groton, CT	8 Ballistic Missile Submarines
	16 Attack Submarines
Brooklyn, NY	1 Destroyer
	1 Frigate
Philadelphia, PA	2 Destroyers
Newport News, VA	4 Ballistic Missile Submarines
Norfolk, VA	6 Aircraft Carriers
	1 Battleship
	9 Cruisers
	19 Destroyers
	9 Frigates
	19 Attack Submarines
	Carrier Groups 4 and 8
	Cruiser/Destroyer Group 8
	Destroyer Squadrons 2, 10, 22, 26, and 32
	Submarine Squadrons 6 and 8
Charleston, SC	2 Cruisers
	10 Destroyers
	12 Frigates
	11 Attack Submarines
	18 Ballistic Missile Submarines
	Cruiser/Destroyer Group 2
	Destroyer Squadrons 4, 6, 20, and 36
	Submarine Squadrons 2, 4, and 18
King's Bay, GA	Submarine Squadron 16 (new East Coast SSBN unit)
Mayport, FL	1 Aircraft Carrier
	1 Cruiser
	4 Destroyers
	24 Frigates
	Carrier Group 6
	Cruiser/Destroyer Group 12
	Destroyer Squadrons 12, 14, and 24

Key West, FL	6 PHMs (hydrofoil patrol boats)
	PHM Squadron 2
Pascagoula, MS	1 Destroyer

Sixth Fleet

HQ Gaeta, Italy
(Sixth Fleet ships operating in the Mediterranean are rotated forward from the Second Fleet. But some organizations are permanent, and here they are.)

Holy Loch, Scotland	Submarine Squadron 14
Naples, Italy	Carrier Group 2
La Maddalena, Italy	Submarine Group 8

Pacific Fleet

Third Fleet

HQ Pearl Harbor, HI

San Diego, CA	2 Aircraft Carriers
	11 Cruisers
	22 Destroyers
	20 Frigates
	14 Attack Submarines
	Carrier Groups 1 and 3
	Cruiser/Destroyer Groups 1, 3, and 5
	Destroyer Squadrons 5, 7, 9, 13, 17, 21, 23, and 31.
	Submarine Group 5
	Submarine Squadron 3
Long Beach, CA	1 Battleship
	1 Destroyer
	12 Frigates
	Surface Squadron 1 (Naval Reserve Force)

Alameda, CA	2 Aircraft Carriers 2 Cruisers
Vallejo, CA	6 Attack Submarines
Bangor, WA	4 Ballistic Missile Submarines 1 Attack Submarine
Bremerton, WA	1 Aircraft Carrier 1 Cruiser 3 Attack Submarines Submarine Group 9
Pearl Harbor, HI	1 Cruiser 3 Destroyers 9 Frigates 18 Attack Submarines Destroyer Squadrons 25, 33, and 35 Submarine Squadrons 1 and 7

Seventh Fleet

HQ Yokosuka, Japan

(As in the Sixth Fleet, most elements of the Seventh Fleet are forwarded from U.S.N.-based units, in this case, the Third Fleet. However, the Seventh Fleet does have some units assigned on a permanent basis.)

Agana, Guam	Submarine Squadron 15
Yokosuka, Japan	1 Aircraft Carrier 1 Cruiser 3 Destroyers 4 Frigates Destroyer Squadron 15 Submarine Group 7
Cubi Point, RP	Carrier Group 5
Subic Bay, RP	1 Cruiser

Crew falls in in dress whites as *Joseph Strauss,* an *Adams* class guided missile destroyer, returns to its home port, Pearl Harbor.

Appendix IV
Warships of the USN

Ohio Class Ballistic Missile Submarines

SSBN 726 Ohio	Bangor, WA	P
SSBN 727 Michigan	Bangor, WA	P
SSBN 728 Florida	Bangor, WA	P
SSBN 729 Georgia	Bangor, WA	P
SSBN 730 Henry M. Jackson	Bangor, WA	P
SSBN 731 Alabama	Bangor, WA	P
SSBN 732 Alaska	Bangor, WA	P
SSBN 733 Nevada		

Lafayette Class Ballistic Missile Submarines

SSBN 616 Lafayette	Groton, CT	A
SSBN 617 Alexander Hamilton	Groton, CT	A
SSBN 619 Andrew Jackson	Groton, CT	A
SSBN 620 John Adams	Charleston, SC	A
SSBN 622 James Monroe	Charleston, SC	A
SSBN 623 Nathan Hale	Charleston, SC	A
SSBN 624 Woodrow Wilson	Charleston, SC	A
SSBN 625 Henry Clay	Charleston, SC	A
SSBN 626 Daniel Webster	Groton, CT	A
SSBN 627 James Madison	Charleston, SC	A
SSBN 628 Tecumseh	Newport News, VA	A
SSBN 629 Daniel Boone	Charleston, SC	A
SSBN 630 John C. Calhoun	Charleston, SC	A
SSBN 631 Ulysses S. Grant	Portsmouth, NH	A
SSBN 632 Von Steuben	Charleston, SC	A
SSBN 633 Casimir Pulaski	Charleston, SC	A

SSBN 634 Stonewall Jackson	Charleston, SC	A
SSBN 635 Sam Rayburn	Groton, CT	A
SSBN 636 Nathanael Greene	Groton, CT	A
SSBN 640 Benjamin Franklin	Charleston, SC	A
SSBN 641 Simon Bolivar	Charleston, SC	A
SSBN 642 Kamehameha	Groton, CT	A
SSBN 643 George Bancroft	Charleston, SC	A
SSBN 644 Lewis and Clark	Charleston, SC	A
SSBN 645 James K. Polk	Charleston, SC	A
SSBN 654 George C. Marshall	Groton, CT	A
SSBN 655 Henry L. Stimson	Newport News, VA	A
SSBN 656 George Wash. Carver	Newport News, VA	A
SSBN 657 Francis Scott Key	Newport News, VA	A
SSBN 658 Mariano G. Vallejo	Charleston, SC	A
SSBN 659 Will Rogers	Newport News, VA	A

Los Angeles Class Attack Submarines

SSN 688 Los Angeles	Pearl Harbor, HI	P
SSN 689 Baton Rouge	Norfolk, VA	A
SSN 690 Philadelphia	Groton, CT	A
SSN 691 Memphis	Norfolk, VA	A
SSN 692 Omaha	Pearl Harbor, HI	P
SSN 693 Cincinnati	Norfolk, VA	A
SSN 694 Groton	Groton, CT	A
SSN 695 Birmingham	Norfolk, VA	A
SSN 696 New York City	Pearl Harbor, HI	P
SSN 697 Indianapolis	Pearl Harbor, HI	P
SSN 698 Bremerton	Pearl Harbor, HI	P

SSN 699 *Jacksonville*	Norfolk, VA	A
SSN 700 *Dallas*	Groton, CT	A
SSN 701 *La Jolla*	San Diego, CA	P
SSN 702 *Phoenix*	Norfolk, VA	A
SSN 703 *Boston*	Groton, CT	A
SSN 704 *Baltimore*	Norfolk, VA	A
SSN 705 *City of Corpus Cristi*	Groton, CT	A
SSN 706 *Albuquerque*	Groton, CT	A
SSN 707 *Portsmouth*	Groton, CT	A
SSN 708 *Minneapolis-St. Paul*	Groton, CT	A
SSN 709 *Hyman G. Rickover*		
SSN 710 *Augusta*		
SSN 711 *San Francisco*	Pearl Harbor, HI	P
SSN 712 *Atlanta*	Norfolk, VA	A
SSN 713 *Houston*	San Diego, CA	P
SSN 714 *Norfolk*	Norfolk, VA	A
SSN 715 *Buffalo*	Norfolk, VA	A
SSN 716 *Salt Lake City*		
SSN 717 *Olympia*		
SSN 718 *Honolulu*		
SSN 719 *Providence*		
SSN 720 *Pittsburgh*		
SSN 721 *Chicago*		
SSN 750 *Newport News*		

Sturgeon Class Attack Submarines

SSN 637 *Sturgeon*	Charleston, SC	A
SSN 638 *Whale*	Groton, CT	A
SSN 639 *Tautog*	Pearl Harbor, HI	P
SSN 646 *Grayling*	Charleston, SC	A
SSN 647 *Pogy*	Vallejo, CA	P
SSN 648 *Aspro*	Pearl Harbor, HI	P
SSN 649 *Sunfish*	Charleston, SC	A
SSN 650 *Pargo*	New London, CT	A
SSN 651 *Queenfish*	Pearl Harbor, HI	P
SSN 652 *Puffer*	Pearl Harbor, HI	P
SSN 653 *Ray*	Charleston, SC	A
SSN 660 *Sand Lance*	Charleston, SC	A
SSN 661 *Lapon*	Norfolk, VA	A
SSN 662 *Gurnard*	San Diego, CA	P
SSN 663 *Hammerhead*	Norfolk, VA	A
SSN 664 *Sea Devil*	Charleston, SC	A
SSN 665 *Guitarro*	San Diego, CA	P
SSN 666 *Hawkbill*	Pearl Harbor, HI	P

SSN 667 *Bergall*	Norfolk, VA	A
SSN 668 *Spadefish*	Norfolk, VA	A
SSN 669 *Seahorse*	Charleston, SC	A
SSN 670 *Finback*	Norfolk, VA	A
SSN 672 *Pintado*	San Diego, CA	P
SSN 673 *Flying Fish*	Norfolk, VA	A
SSN 674 *Trepang*	New London, CT	A
SSN 675 *Bluefish*	Norfolk, VA	A
SSN 676 *Billfish*	New London, CT	A
SSN 677 *Drum*	San Diego, CA	P
SSN 678 *Archerfish*	Portsmouth, NH	A
SSN 679 *Silversides*	Norfolk, VA	A
SSN 680 *William H. Bates*	San Diego, CA	P
SSN 681 *Batfish*	Charleston, SC	A
SSN 682 *Tunny*	Pearl Harbor, HI	P
SSN 683 *Parche*	Vallejo, CA	P
SSN 684 *Cavalla*	Pearl Harbor, HI	P
SSN 686 *L. Mendel Rivers*	Charleston, SC	A
SSN 687 *Richard B. Russell*	Vallejo, CA	P

Narwhal Class Attack Submarine

SSN 671 *Narwhal*	Charleston, SC	A

Glenard P. Lipscomb Class Attack Submarine

SSN 685 *Glenard P. Lipscomb*	Norfolk, VA	A

Permit Class Attack Submarines

SSN 594 *Permit*	Vallejo, CA	P
SSN 595 *Plunger*	San Diego, CA	P
SSN 596 *Barb*	San Diego, CA	P
SSN 603 *Pollack*	San Diego, CA	P
SSN 604 *Haddo*	San Diego, CA	P
SSN 605 *Jack*	Portsmouth, NH	A
SSN 606 *Tinosa*	Portsmouth, NH	A
SSN 607 *Dace*	New London, CT	A
SSN 612 *Guardfish*	Vallejo, CA	P
SSN 613 *Flasher*	Vallejo, CA	P
SSN 614 *Greenling*	New London, CT	A
SSN 615 *Gato*	New London, CT	A
SSN 621 *Haddock*	San Diego, CA	P

Skipjack Class Attack Submarines

SSN 585 *Skipjack*	Groton, CT	A
SSN 588 *Scamp*	Groton, CT	A
SSN 590 *Sculpin*	Groton, CT	A
SSN 591 *Shark*	Groton, CT	A
SSN 592 *Snook*	Groton, CT	A

Skate Class Attack Submarines

SSN 578 *Skate*	Pearl Harbor, HI	P
SSN 579 *Swordfish*	Pearl Harbor, HI	P
SSN 583 *Sargo*	Pearl Harbor, HI	P
SSN 584 *Seadragon*	Pearl Harbor, HI	P

Seawolf Class Attack Submarine

SSN 575 *Seawolf*	Sasebo, Japan	P

Barbel Class Attack Submarines

SS 580 *Barbel*	Pearl Harbor, HI	P
SS 581 *Blueback*	San Diego, CA	P
SS 582 *Bonefish*	Charleston, SC	A

Darter Class Attack Submarine

SS 576 *Darter*	Sasebo, Japan	

Midway Class Aircraft Carriers

CV 41 *Midway*	Yokosuka, Japan	P
CV 43 *Coral Sea*	Norfolk, VA	A

Forrestal Class Aircraft Carriers

CV 59 *Forrestal*	Norfolk, VA	A
CV 60 *Saratoga*	Mayport, FL	A
CV 61 *Ranger*	San Diego, CA	P
CV 62 *Independence*	Norfolk, VA	A

Kitty Hawk Class Aircraft Carriers

CV 63 *Kitty Hawk*	San Diego, CA	P
CV 64 *Constellation*	San Diego, CA	P
CV 66 *America*	Norfolk, VA	A
CV 67 *John F. Kennedy*	Norfolk, VA	A

Enterprise Class Aircraft Carrier

CVN 65 *Enterprise*	Alameda, CA	P

Nimitz Class Aircraft Carriers

CVN 68 *Nimitz*	Norfolk, VA	A
CVN 69 *Dwight D. Eisenhower*	Norfolk, VA	A
CVN 70 *Carl Vinson*	Alameda, CA	P
CVN 71 *Theodore Roosevelt*	Alameda, CA	P
CVN 72 *Abraham Lincoln*		
CVN 73 *George Washington*		

Iowa Class Battleships

BB 61 *Iowa*	Staten Island, NY	A
BB 62 *New Jersey*	Long Beach, CA	P
BB 63 *Missouri*	San Francisco, CA	P
BB 64 *Wisconsin*		A

Ticonderoga Class Guided Missile Cruisers

CG 47 *Ticonderoga*	Norfolk, VA	A
CG 48 *Yorktown*		
CG 49 *Vincennes*		
CG 50 *Valley Forge*		
CG 51 *Thomas S. Gates*		
CG 52 *Bunker Hill*		

Virginia Class Guided Missile Cruisers

CGN 38 *Virginia*	Norfolk, VA	A
CGN 39 *Texas*	San Diego, CA	P
CGN 40 *Mississippi*	Norfolk, VA	A
CGN 41 *Arkansas*	Alameda, CA	P

California Class Guided Missile Cruisers

CGN 36 *California*	Alameda, CA	P
CGN 37 *South Carolina*	Norfolk, VA	A

Long Beach Class Guided Missile Cruiser

CGN 9 *Long Beach*	San Diego, CA	P

Belknap Class Guided Missile Cruisers

CG 26 *Belknap*	Norfolk, VA	A
CG 27 *Josephus Daniels*	Norfolk, VA	A
CG 28 *Wainwright*	Charleston, SC	A
CG 29 *Jouett*	San Diego, CA	P
CG 30 *Horne*	San Diego, CA	P
CG 31 *Sterett*	Subic Bay, RP	P
CG 32 *William H. Standley*	San Diego, CA	P
CG 33 *Fox*	Long Beach, CA	P
CG 34 *Biddle*	Norfolk, VA	A
CGN 35 *Truxtun*	Bremerton, WA	P

Leahy Class Guided Missile Cruisers

CG 16 *Leahy*	San Diego, CA	P
CG 17 *Harry E. Yarnell*	Norfolk, VA	A
CG 18 *Worden*	Pearl Harbor, HI	P
CG 19 *Dale*	Mayport, FL	A
CG 20 *Richmond K. Turner*	Charleston, SC	A
CG 21 *Gridley*	San Diego, CA	P
CG 22 *England*	San Diego, CA	P
CG 23 *Halsey*	San Diego, CA	P
CG 24 *Reeves*	Yokosuka, Japan	P
CGN 25 *Bainbridge*	Bremerton, WA	P

Charles F. Adams Class Guided Missile Destroyers

DDG 2 *Charles F. Adams*	Mayport, FL	A
DDG 3 *John Keene*	Norfolk, VA	A
DDG 4 *Lawrence*	Norfolk, VA	A
DDG 5 *Claude V. Ricketts*	Norfolk, VA	A
DDG 6 *Barney*	Norfolk, VA	A
DDG 7 *Henry B. Wilson*	San Diego, CA	P
DDG 8 *Lynde McCormick*	San Diego, CA	P
DDG 9 *Towers*	Yokosuka, Japan	P
DDG 10 *Sampson*	Mayport, FL	A
DDG 11 *Sellers*	Charleston, SC	A
DDG 12 *Robison*	San Diego, CA	P
DDG 13 *Hoel*	Long Beach, CA	P
DDG 14 *Buchanan*	San Diego, CA	P
DDG 15 *Berkeley*	San Diego, CA	P
DDG 16 *Joseph Strauss*	Pearl Harbor, HI	P
DDG 17 *Conyngham*	Norfolk, VA	A
DDG 18 *Semmes*	Charleston, SC	A
DDG 19 *Tattnall*	Mayport, FL	A
DDG 20 *Goldsborough*	Pearl Harbor, HI	P
DDG 21 *Cochrane*	Yokosuka, Japan	P
DDG 22 *Benjamin Stoddert*	Pearl Harbor, HI	P
DDG 23 *Richard E. Byrd*	Norfolk, VA	A
DDG 24 *Waddell*	San Diego, CA	P

Coontz Class Guided Missile Destroyers

DDG 37 *Farragut*	Philadelphia, PA	A
DDG 38 *Luce*	Mayport, FL	A
DDG 39 *MacDonough*	Charleston, SC	A
DDG 40 *Coontz*	Norfolk, VA	A
DDG 41 *King*	Norfolk, VA	A
DDG 42 *Mahan*	Charleston, SC	A
DDG 43 *Dahlgren*	Philadelphia, PA	A
DDG 44 *William V. Pratt*	Charleston, SC	A
DDG 45 *Dewey*	Charleston, SC	A
DDG 46 *Preble*	Norfolk, VA	A

Arleigh Burke Class Guided Missile Destroyers

DDG 51 *Arleigh Burke*		

Kidd Class Guided Missile Destroyers

DDG 993 *Kidd*	Norfolk, VA	A
DDG 994 *Callaghan*	San Diego, CA	P
DDG 995 *Scott*	Norfolk, VA	A
DDG 996 *Chandler*	San Diego, CA	P

Spruance Class Destroyers

DD 963 *Spruance*	Norfolk, VA	A
DD 964 *Paul F. Foster*	Long Beach, CA	P

DD 965 *Kinkaid*	San Diego, CA	P
DD 966 *Hewitt*	San Diego, CA	P
DD 967 *Elliot*	San Diego, CA	P
DD 968 *Arthur W. Radford*	Norfolk, VA	A
DD 969 *Peterson*	Norfolk, VA	A
DD 970 *Caron*	Norfolk, VA	A
DD 971 *David R. Ray*	San Diego, CA	P
DD 972 *Oldenford*	San Diego, CA	P
DD 973 *John Young*	San Diego, CA	P
DD 974 *Comte de Grasse*	Pascagoula, MS	A
DD 975 *O'Brien*	San Diego, CA	P
DD 976 *Merrill*	San Diego, CA	P
DD 977 *Briscoe*	Norfolk, VA	A
DD 978 *Stump*	Brooklyn, NY	A
DD 979 *Conolly*	Portland, ME	A
DD 980 *Moosbrugger*	Charleston, SC	A
DD 981 *John Hancock*	Charleston, SC	A
DD 982 *Nicholson*	Charleston, SC	A
DD 983 *John Rodgers*	Charleston, SC	A
DD 984 *Leftwich*	San Diego, CA	P
DD 985 *Cushing*	San Diego, CA	P
DD 986 *Harry W. Hill*	San Diego, CA	P
DD 987 *O'Bannon*	Charleston, SC	A
DD 988 *Thorn*	Charleston, SC	A
DD 989 *Deyo*	Charleston, SC	A
DD 990 *Ingersoll*	San Diego, CA	P
DD 991 *Fife*	San Diego, CA	P
DD 992 *Fletcher*	San Diego, CA	P
DD 997 *Hayler*	Norfolk, VA	A

Brooke Class Guided Missile Frigates

FFG 1 *Brooke*	San Diego, CA	P
FFG 2 *Ramsey*	Long Beach, CA	P
FFG 3 *Schofield*	San Diego, CA	P
FFG 4 *Talbot*	Mayport, FL	A
FFG 5 *Richard L. Page*	Mayport, FL	A
FFG 6 *Julius A. Furer*	Charleston, SC	A

Oliver Hazard Perry Class Guided Missile Frigates

FFG 7 *Oliver Hazard Perry*	Mayport, FL	A
FFG 8 *McInerney*	Mayport, FL	A
FFG 9 *Wadsworth*	Long Beach, CA	P
FFG 10 *Duncan*		
FFG 11 *Clark*	Mayport, FL	A
FFG 12 *George Philip*	San Diego, CA	P
FFG 13 *Samuel Eliot Morison*	Mayport, FL	A
FFG 14 *Sides*	San Diego, CA	P
FFG 15 *Estocin*	Mayport, FL	A
FFG 16 *Clifton Sprague*	Mayport, FL	A
FFG 19 *John A. Moore*	San Diego, CA	P
FFG 20 *Antrim*	Mayport, FL	A
FFG 21 *Flatley*	Mayport, FL	A
FFG 22 *Fahrion*	Mayport, FL	A
FFG 23 *Lewis B. Puller*	San Diego, CA	P
FFG 24 *Jack Williams*	Mayport, FL	A
FFG 25 *Copeland*	Long Beach, CA	P
FFG 26 *Gallery*	Mayport, FL	P
FFG 27 *Mahlon S. Tinsdale*	San Diego, CA	P
FFG 28 *Boone*	Mayport, FL	A
FFG 29 *Stephen W. Groves*	Mayport, FL	A
FFG 30 *Reid*	San Diego, CA	P
FFG 31 *Stark*	Mayport, FL	A
FFG 32 *John L. Hall*	Mayport, FL	A
FFG 33 *Jarrett*	Long Beach, CA	P
FFG 34 *Aubrey Fitch*	Mayport, FL	A
FFG 36 *Underwood*	Mayport, FL	A
FFG 37 *Crommelin*	Long Beach, CA	P
FFG 38 *Curts*	Long Beach, CA	P
FFG 39 *Doyle*	Mayport, FL	A
FFG 40 *Halyburton*	Charleston, SC	A
FFG 41 *McCluskey*	Long Beach, CA	P
FFG 42 *Klakring*	Charleston, SC	A
FFG 43 *Thach*	Long Beach, CA	P
FFG 45 *De Wert*	Charleston, SC	A
FFG 46 *Rentz*		
FFG 47 *Nicholas*	Charleston, SC	A
FFG 48 *Vandergrift*		
FFG 49 *Robert C. Bradley*		
FFG 50 *Taylor*		
FFG 51 *Gary*		
FFG 52 *Carr*		
FFG 53 *Hawes*		
FFG 54 *Ford*		
FFG 55 *Elrod*		
FFG 56 *Simpson*		
FFG 57 *Reuben James*		
FFG 58 *Samuel B. Roberts*		
FFG 59 *Kauffman*		
FFG 60 *Rodney M. Davis*		

Glover Class Frigate

FF 1098 *Glover*	Norfolk, VA	A

Knox Class Frigates

FF 1052 *Knox*	Yokosuka, Japan	P
FF 1053 *Roark*	San Diego, CA	P
FF 1054 *Gray*		
FF 1055 *Hepburn*	San Diego, CA	P
FF 1056 *Connole*	Newport, RI	A
FF 1057 *Rathburne*	Pearl Harbor, HI	P
FF 1058 *Meyerkord*	Long Beach, CA	P
FF 1059 *W. S. Sims*	Mayport, FL	A
FF 1060 *Lang*		
FF 1061 *Patterson*		
FF 1062 *Whipple*	Pearl Harbor, HI	P
FF 1063 *Reasoner*	San Diego, CA	P
FF 1064 *Lockwood*	Yokosuka, Japan	P
FF 1065 *Stein*	San Diego, CA	P
FF 1066 *Marvin Shields*	San Diego, CA	P
FF 1067 *Francis Hammond*	Yokosuka, Japan	P
FF 1068 *Vreeland*	Mayport, FL	A
FF 1069 *Bagley*	San Diego, CA	P
FF 1070 *Downes*	San Diego, CA	P
FF 1071 *Badger*	Pearl Harbor, HI	P
FF 1072 *Blakely*		
FF 1073 *Robert E. Peary*	Pearl Harbor, HI	P
FF 1074 *Harold E. Holt*	Pearl Harbor, HI	P
FF 1075 *Trippe*	Charleston, SC	A
FF 1076 *Fanning*	San Diego, CA	P
FF 1077 *Ouellet*	Pearl Harbor, HI	P
FF 1078 *Joseph Hewes*	Charleston, SC	A
FF 1079 *Bowen*	Charleston, SC	A
FF 1080 *Paul*	Mayport, FL	A
FF 1081 *Aylwin*	Charleston, SC	A
FF 1082 *Elmer Montgomery*	Mayport, FL	A
FF 1083 *Cook*	San Diego, CA	P
FF 1084 *McCandless*	Norfolk, VA	A
FF 1085 *Donald B. Beary*	Norfolk, VA	A
FF 1086 *Brewton*	Pearl Harbor, HI	P
FF 1087 *Kirk*	Yokosuka, Japan	P
FF 1088 *Barbey*	Long Beach, CA	P
FF 1089 *Jesse L. Brown*	Boston, MA	A
FF 1090 *Ainsworth*	Charleston, SC	A
FF 1091 *Miller*		
FF 1092 *Thomas C. Hart*	Norfolk, VA	A
FF 1093 *Capodanno*	Newport, RI	A
FF 1094 *Pharris*	Brooklyn, NY	A
FF 1095 *Truett*	Norfolk, VA	A
FF 1096 *Valdez*		
FF 1097 *Moinester*	Norfolk, VA	A

Garcia Class Frigates

FF 1040 *Garcia*	Charleston, SC	A
FF 1041 *Bradley*	Long Beach, CA	P
FF 1043 *Edward McDonnell*	Mayport, FL	A
FF 1044 *Brumby*	Charleston, SC	A
FF 1045 *Davidson*	Pearl Harbor, HI	P
FF 1047 *Voge*	Mayport, FL	A
FF 1048 *Sample*	Pearl Harbor, HI	P
FF 1049 *Koelsch*	Mayport, FL	A
FF 1050 *Albert David*	San Diego, CA	P
FF 1051 *O'Callahan*	San Diego, CA	P

Bronstein Class Frigates

FF 1037 *Bronstein*	San Diego, CA	P
FF 1038 *McCloy*	Norfolk, VA	A

Blue Ridge Class Amphibious Command Ships

LCC 19 *Blue Ridge*	Yokosuka, Japan	P
LCC 20 *Mount Whitney*	Norfolk, VA	A

Wasp Class Amphibious Assault Ship

LHD 1 *Wasp*		

Tarawa Class Amphibious Assault Ships

LHA 1 *Tarawa*	San Diego, CA	P
LHA 2 *Siapan*	Norfolk, VA	A
LHA 3 *Belleau Wood*	San Diego, CA	P
LHA 4 *Nassau*	Norfolk, VA	A
LHA 5 *Peleliu*	Long Beach, CA	P

Iwo Jima Class Amphibious Assault Ships

LPH 2 *Iwo Jima*	Norfolk, VA	A
LPH 3 *Okinawa*	San Diego, CA	P
LPH 7 *Guadalcanal*	Norfolk, VA	A
LPH 9 *Guam*	Norfolk, VA	A
LPH 10 *Tripoli*	San Diego, CA	P
LPH 11 *New Orleans*	San Diego, CA	P
LPH 12 *Inchon*	Norfolk, VA	A

Raleigh Class Amphibious Transport Docks

LPD 1 *Raleigh*	Norfolk, VA	A
LPD 2 *Vancouver*	San Diego, CA	P

Austin Class Amphibious Transport Docks

LPD 4 *Austin*	Norfolk, VA	A
LPD 5 *Ogdon*	Long Beach, CA	P
LPD 6 *Duluth*	San Diego, CA	P
LPD 7 *Cleveland*	San Diego, CA	P
LPD 8 *Dubuque*	San Diego, CA	P
LPD 9 *Denver*	San Diego, CA	P
LPD 10 *Juneau*	San Diego, CA	P
LPD 12 *Shreveport*	Norfolk, VA	A
LPD 13 *Nashville*	Norfolk, VA	A
LPD 14 *Trenton*	Norfolk, VA	A
LPD 15 *Ponce*	Norfolk, VA	A

Thomaston Class Landing Ship Docks

LSD 28 *Thomaston*	San Diego, CA	P
LSD 30 *Fort Snelling*	Norfolk, VA	A
LSD 32 *Spiegel Grove*	Norfolk, VA	A
LSD 33 *Alamo*	San Diego, CA	P
LSD 34 *Hermitage*	Norfolk, VA	A
LSD 35 *Monticello*	San Diego, CA	P

Anchorage Class Landing Ship Docks

LSD 36 *Anchorage*	San Diego, CA	P
LSD 37 *Portland*	Norfolk, VA	A
LSD 38 *Pensacola*	Norfolk, VA	A

LSD 39 *Mount Vernon*	San Diego, CA	P
LSD 40 *Fort Fisher*	San Diego, CA	P

Whidbey Island Class Landing Ship Docks

LSD 41 *Whidbey Island*	
LSD 42 *Germantown*	

Newport Class Landing Ship Tank

LST 1179 *Newport*	Norfolk, VA	A
LST 1180 *Manitowoc*	Norfolk, VA	A
LST 1181 *Sumter*	Norfolk, VA	A
LST 1182 *Fresno*	San Diego, CA	P
LST 1183 *Peoria*	San Diego, CA	P
LST 1184 *Frederick*	San Diego, CA	P
LST 1185 *Schenectady*	San Diego, CA	P
LST 1186 *Cayuga*	San Diego, CA	P
LST 1187 *Tuscaloosa*	San Diego, CA	P
LST 1188 *Saginaw*	Portsmouth, VA	A
LST 1189 *San Bernardino*	San Diego, CA	P
LST 1192 *Spartanburg County*	Norfolk, VA	A
LST 1193 *Fairfax County*	Norfolk, VA	A
LST 1194 *La Moure County*	Norfolk, VA	A
LST 1195 *Barbour County*	San Diego, CA	P
LST 1196 *Harlan County*	Norfolk, VA	A
LST 1197 *Barnstable County*	Norfolk, VA	A
LST 1198 *Bristol County*	San Diego, CA	P

Charleston Class Amphibious Cargo Ships

LKA 113 *Charleston*	Norfolk, VA	A
LKA 114 *Durham*	San Diego, CA	P
LKA 115 *Mobile*	Long Beach, CA	P
LKA 116 *Saint Louis*	Sasebo, Japan	P
LKA 117 *El Paso*	Norfolk, VA	A

Avenger Class Mine Countermeasures Ships

MCM 1 *Avenger*
MCM 2 *Defender*
MCM 3 *Sentry*
MCM 4 *Champion*
MCM 5 *Guardian*

Cardinal Class Minesweeper/Hunter

MSH 1 *Cardinal*

Aggressive Class Ocean Minesweepers

MSO 443 *Fidelity*	Panama City, FL	A
MSO 448 *Illusive*	Charleston, SC	A
MSO 490 *Leader*	Charleston, SC	A

Suribachi Class Ammunition Ships

AE 21 *Suribachi*	Earle, NJ	A
AE 22 *Mauna Kea*	Vallejo, CA	P

Nitro Class Ammunition Ships

AE 23 *Nitro*	Earle, NJ	A
AE 24 *Pyro*	Vallejo, CA	P
AE 25 *Haleakala*	Concord, CA	P

Kilauea Class Ammunition Ships

TAE 26 *Kilauea*		
AE 27 *Butte*	Earle, NJ	A
AE 28 *Santa Barbara*	Charleston, SC	A
AE 29 *Mount Hood*	Concord, CA	P
AE 32 *Flint*	Concord, CA	P
AE 33 *Shasta*	San Diego, CA	P
AE 34 *Mount Baker*	Charleston, SC	A
AE 35 *Kiska*	Concord, CA	P

Mars Class Combat Stores Ships

AFS 1 *Mars*	Oakland, CA	P
AFS 2 *Sylvania*	Norfolk, VA	A
AFS 3 *Niagara Falls*	Guam, HI	P
AFS 4 *White Plains*	Yokosuka, Japan	P
AFS 5 *Concord*	Norfolk, VA	A
AFS 6 *San Diego*	Norfolk, VA	A
AFS 7 *San Jose*	Agana, Guam	P

Improved Cimarron Class Oilers

AO 98 *Caloosahatchee*	Norfolk, VA	A
AO 99 *Canisteo*	Norfolk, VA	A

Cimarron Class Oilers

AO 177 *Cimarron*	Pearl Harbor, HI	P
AO 178 *Monongahela*	Norfolk, VA	A
AO 179 *Merrimack*	Norfolk, VA	A
AO 180 *Willamette*	Pearl Harbor, HI	P
AO 186 *Platte*	Norfolk, VA	A

Sacramento Class Fast Combat Support Ships

AOE 1 *Sacramento*	Bremerton, WA	P
AOE 2 *Camden*	Bremerton, WA	P
AOE 3 *Seattle*	Norfolk, VA	A
AOE 4 *Detroit*	Norfolk, VA	A

Wichita Class Fleet Oilers

AOR 1 *Wichita*	Alameda, CA	P
AOR 2 *Milwaukee*	Norfolk, VA	A
AOR 3 *Kansas City*	Alameda, CA	P
AOR 4 *Savannah*	Norfolk, VA	A
AOR 5 *Wabash*	Alameda, CA	P
AOR 6 *Kalamazoo*	Norfolk, VA	A
AOR 7 *Roanoke*	Alameda, CA	P

Rigel Class Stores Ship

TAF 58 *Rigel*

Sirius Class Combat Stores Ships

TAFS 8 *Sirius*		
TAFS 9 *Spica*	Oakland, CA	P
TAFS 10 *Saturn*		

Mispillion Class Oilers

TAO 105 *Mispillion*
TAO 106 *Navasota*
TAO 107 *Passumpsic*
TAO 108 *Pawkatuck*
TAO 109 *Waccamaw*

Neosho Class Oilers

TAO 143 *Neosho*
TAO 144 *Mississinewa*
TAO 145 *Hassayampa*
TAO 146 *Kawishiwi*
TAO 147 *Truckee*
TAO 148 *Ponchatoula*

Dixie Class Destroyer Tenders

AD 15 *Prairie*	Long Beach, CA	P
AD 18 *Sierra*	Charleston, SC	A
AD 19 *Yosemite*	Mayport, FL	A

Samuel Gompers Class Destroyer Tenders

AD 37 *Samuel Gompers*	San Diego, CA	P
AD 38 *Puget Sound*	Gaeta, Italy	A

Yellowstone Class Destroyer Tenders

AD 41 *Yellowstone*	Norfolk, VA	A
AD 42 *Acadia*	San Diego, CA	P
AD 43 *Cape Cod*	San Diego, CA	P
AD 44 *Shenandoah*	Norfolk, VA	A

Ajax Class Repair Ships

AR 5 *Vulcan*	Norfolk, VA	A
AR 6 *Ajax*	San Diego, CA	P
AR 7 *Hector*	Oakland, CA	P
AR 8 *Jason*	Pearl Harbor, HI	P

Fulton/Proteus Class Submarine Tenders

AS 11 *Fulton*	Quincy, MA	A
AS 18 *Orion*	La Maddalena, Italy	A
AS 19 *Proteus*	Agana, Guam	P

L.Y. Spear/Emory S. Land Class Submarine Tenders

AS 36 *L. Y. Spear*	Norfolk, VA	A
AS 37 *Dixon*	San Diego, CA	P
AS 39 *Emory S. Land*	Norfolk, VA	A
AS 40 *Frank Cable*	Charleston, SC	A
AS 41 *McKee*	San Diego, CA	P

MK-54 five-inch gun.

Appendix V

U.S.N. Carrier Air Wings

The Typical Carrier Air Wing

To begin with, there is no such thing as a typical carrier air wing. The present standard has been around for a while, but the numbers and types of aircraft on the carriers are constantly changing as planes age and new ones come into fleet service. For example, the older carriers—*Coral Sea* and *Midway*—cannot handle F-14s and S-3s. And the types of aircraft on the ship can be shuffled to account for various contingencies; *John F. Kennedy,* off Lebanon, carried an experimental attack component comprised solely of A-6s.

That said, here's a look at a "typical" USN air wing:

Modex	Designation	Type	Number Carried	Trim Color	Notes
100	VF (fighter)	F-14	12	Red	Also Marine F-4s to be replaced by F-18s.
200	VF (fighter)	F-14	12	Yellow	
300	VA (light attack)	A-7	12	Blue	To be replaced by F-18s.
400	VA (light attack)	A-7	12	Orange	
500	VA (medium attack)	A-6	10	Green	Also 4 KA-6Ds
600	VAW (airborne early warning)	E-2	4	Black	
	VAQ (electronic warfare)	EA-6	4	Black	Also EA-3s on forward carriers
700	VS (fixed-wing antisub)	S-3	10	Black	
	HS (helicopter)	SH-3	6	Black	

Current Carrier Air Wings

Navy carrier air wings are hard to pin down. Some squadrons stay together constantly through deployments (and often with the same ship—CVW-8 is the only wing *Nimitz* has ever had). Others, such as the Navy's precious electronic warfare assets, flit from ship to ship seemingly without a rest.

This list is a representative sampling from early 1985, seeking to match carriers to CVWs. Not all these wings were embarked then. Some had just returned from deployment. Others were getting ready to sail. There are also two reserve carrier air wings, CVWR-20 on the East Coast and CVWR-30 on the West Coast. Reserve squadrons do not normally embark as a wing and are not included here.

CVW-1/AB
USS *America* (CV 66)
VF-33	Tarsiers
VF-102	Diamondbacks
VA-46	Clansmen
VA-72	Bluehawks
VA-34	Blue Blasters
VAQ-136	Gauntlets
VAW-123	Screwtops
VS-32	Yellow Tails
HS-11	Dragon Slayers

CVW-2/NE
USS *Ranger* (CV-61)
VF-1	Wolfpack
VF-2	Bounty Hunters
VA-146	Blue Diamonds
VA-147	Argonauts
VA-145	Swordsmen
VAQ-130	Zappers
VAW-116	Sun Kings
VS-38	Red Griffins
HS-2	Golden Falcons

CVW-3/AC
USS *John F. Kennedy* (CV-67)
VF-11	Red Rippers
VF-31	Tomcatters
VA-75	Sunday Punchers
VA-85	Bombing Buckeyes
VAQ-137	Rooks
VAW-126	Seahawks
VS-22	Checkmates
HS-7	Shamrocks

CVW-5/NF
USS *Midway* (CV 41)
VF-151	Vigilantes
VF-161	Chargers
VA-93	Ravens
VA-56	Champions
VA-115	Eagles
VAQ-136	Gauntlets
VAW-115	Liberty Bells
HS-12	Wyverns

CVW-6/AE
USS *Independence* (CV 62)
VF-14	Tophatters
VF-32	Swordsmen
VA-87	Golden Warriors
VA-15	Valions
VA-176	Thunderbolts
VAQ-131	Lancers
VAW-122	Steeljaws
VS-28	Hukkers
HS-15	Red Lions

CVW-7/AG
USS *Dwight D. Eisenhower* (CV 69)
VF-142	Ghostriders
VF-143	Pukin' Dogs
VA-66	Waldos
VA-12	Clinchers
VA-65	Tigers
VAQ-132	Scorpions
VAW-121	Bluetails
VS-31	Topcats
HS-5	Night Dippers

CVW-8/AJ
USS *Nimitz* (CV 68)
VF-41	Black Aces

VF-84   Jolly Rogers
VA-82   Marauders
VA-86   Sidewinders
VA-35   Black Panthers
VAQ-135   Ravens
VAW-124   Bear Aces
VS-24   Scouts
HS-9   Sea Griffins

CVW-9/NG
USS *Kitty Hawk* (CV-63)
VF-24   Fighting Renegades
VF-211   Checkmates
VA-192   Golden Dragons
VA-195   Dam Busters
VA-165   Boomers
VAQ-138   Yellowjackets
VAW-112   Golden Hawks
VS-33   Screwbirds
HS-8   Eight Ballers

CVW-11/NH
USS *Enterprise* (CV-65)
VF-114   Aardvarks
VF-213   Black Lions
VA-22   Fighting Redcocks
VA-94   Mighty Shrikes
VA-95   Green Lizards
VAQ-133   Wizards
VAW-117   Night Hawks
VS-21   Redtails
HS-6   Indians

CVW-13/AK
USS *Coral Sea* (CV-43)
VFA-131   Wildcats
VFA-132   Privateers
VMFA-314   Black Knights
VMFA-323   Death Rattlers
VA-55   Warhorses
VAQ-139   Cougars
VAW-127   Seabats
HS-17   Neptune's Raiders

CVW-14/NK
USS *Constellation* (CV-64)

Crewmen on a carrier line up another cat shot.

VF-21   Freelancers
VF-154   Black Knights
VFA-25   Fist of the Fleet
VFA-113   Stingers
VA-196   Milestones
VAQ-139   Cougars
VAW-113   Black Eagles
VS-37   Roostertails
HS-8   Eightballers

CVW-15/NL
USS *Carl Vinson* (CV-70)
VF-51   Screaming Eagles
VF-111   Sundowners
VA-27   Chargers
VA-97   Warhawks
VA-52   Knightriders
VAQ-134   Garudas
VAW-114   Hormel Hawgs
VS-29   Dragonfires
HS-4   Black Knights

CVW-17/AA
USS *Saratoga* (CV-60)
VF-103   Sluggers
VF-74   Be-Devilers
VA-83   Rampagers
VA-81   Sunliners
VMA
(AW)-533   Hawks
VMAQ-2   Det
VAW-125   Tigertails
VS-30   Diamond Cutters
HS-3   Tridents

America (CV-66).

Air Wing Crew

On board the carrier, the crew is divided almost equally between the ship's company and the air wing. The air department—the part of the ship's company that works on the flight and hangar decks —is grouped into four divisions:

V-1 handles the planes on the flight deck.
V-2 mans the catapults and arresting gear.
V-3 handles the planes on the hangar deck.
V-4 is in charge of refueling the planes.

The flight deck personnel can be distinguished by the colors and trim of the jerseys they must wear on duty:

Blue—Plane pushers, chockmen
Blue with white "T"—Tractor drivers
Blue with white trim—Elevator operators

Yellow—Plane handling officers, arresting gear and catapult officers
Green with black letter—Arresting-gear and catapult crewmen
Green with squadron numbers—Maintenance personnel
Green with white trim—Plane inspectors
Green—Marine guards, flight deck visitors
Red with black stripe—Ordnance personnel
Red with black letter—Damage control crewmen
Purple—Fueling crews
Brown—Plane captains
White—Flight surgeon
White with red cross—Medical corpsmen
White with blue trim—Messengers
Silver—"Hot suit" fire rescue personnel

Appendix VI
Birdwatchers' Guide: Navy Camouflage and Aircraft Markings

Navy Camouflage

The new gray-on-gray Navy camouflage gives new meaning to the phrase "ton of bricks"—planes slamming on the decks now look as if they're molded from solid concrete. Although some Navy pilots resisted the change, they were converted after seeing how the new schemes worked out in mock combat. Then they couldn't wait until their own aircraft received the new toned-down look, thus proving the old fighter pilot admonition: "Never fly in an aircraft that isn't camouflaged!"

The new color schemes are the first real change in naval aircraft finishes since the Navy switched from blue to gull gray with light undersides, although the fleet *did* switch from flat gull gray to glossy gull gray in 1971. Big deal. The light gray finish was a good compromise between the high visibility needed for carrier ops and the lower visibility needed for war at sea. But for air-to-air fighting and attacks against ground targets, the gray Navy birds with their bright plumage of squadron markings made easy targets.

The Navy experimented with the Air Force-style camouflage for Intruders, Skyhawks, and Vigilantes during the Vietnam war, but the tests conducted on *Kitty Hawk* and *Constellation* in 1966 proved unsuccessful for two reasons. First, as long as the aircraft was right side up, the scheme worked fine. But if the plane was bounced from above, a break turn would expose the aircraft's white belly, easily spotted against the dark earth.

Fire from the ground produced similar problems. Evasive action exposed the dark upper surfaces against the lighter sky, making the gunner's job easier.

The Air Force eventually compromised by wrapping the three-tone camouflage around the underside of the aircraft as well. But the darker finish never caught on with the Navy because it increased the danger already inherent in night carrier landings. The fleet continued the light gray scheme well into the seventies, until the now infamous AIMVAL-ACEVAL jousts at Nellis AFB in Nevada.

The exercises, while not exactly no-holds-barred, were quite extensive and proved a number of crucial but long forgotten air combat concepts. One of these was the relationship of size to survivability. Both services' pet fighters, the F-15 and the F-14, were at a disadvantage in close-in dogfights against the smaller F-5s and F-16s.

The Tomcat's bright colors and garish markings only made the situation worse. The Navy showed up with half a dozen F-14s finished in the new Ferris "splinter" camouflage. Developed by aviation artist Keith Ferris from experimental World War II Luftwaffe design, the ragged light-and-dark scheme helped disguise the aircraft's attitude by scrambling the shadows pilots use as visual cues. There was even a false canopy painted over the forward landing gear doors.

The Ferris scheme was not adopted by the Navy or the Air Force. Instead, the fleet adopted the now familiar low-contrast gray and gray scheme introduced by the Air Force. There were a number of "free-lance," low-viz Navy designs in the late seventies, before the Naval Air Systems Command stepped in to standardize a low visibility paint scheme for attack aircraft.

NavAirSysCom's Air Combat Survivability Branch developed the new camouflage using computer modeling techniques and flight tests. The computer predicted the amount of reflectivity needed in the paint to accurately match different backgrounds. Higher-reflectance translates into lighter colors to the eyes, but special qualities in the paint enable the finish to appear to change hue. For example, the underside of low-viz aircraft appears almost white at high noon, but seems to darken to a pearly gray at sundown.

Close attention was paid to lightening the finish where shadows are normally thrown in flight, to give the aircraft an overall solid gray appearance. There are actually four such finishes, optimized for use in central Europe, northern Europe, Southeast Asia, and the Middle East. The scheme adopted for the fleet is a compromised "all-purpose" camouflage, but finishes for specific contingencies have also been developed.

The new tactical paint schemes do work. Prowler drivers, used to having their big EA-6B spotted as far out as thirty miles, now say they can get within five miles of the bad guys without being seen. But there are minor problems. The new faded finishes fade even quicker in the harsh environment of blue water. The multi-million dollar matte jets look pretty washed out at the end of a long cruise.

In contrast, the glossy finish on the E-2s and S-3s keep them looking good. But not for long —low-viz camouflage for the Hawkeyes and Vikings is on its way. In fact, every carrier aircraft in the fleet—except for some helicopters—is scheduled for the new slate-gray paint jobs. The change will come gradually, as the aircraft are overhauled during scheduled progressive air rework at the Naval Rework Facilities. One admiral, exasperated by the disappearance of the beloved squadron markings, proposed painting the full color badges and ribbons on the wing's four KA-6 tankers, but someone—probably the tanker crews—nixed the idea.

The markings aren't gone forever. They're just toned down, along with the aircraft finish. Research found that the bright markings were not just easy for the eye to detect, but that the red ejection triangles and intake warnings also made it easier for today's ultra-sensitive infrared missiles to get an IR "paint" on Navy aircraft.

So the warning panels, along with the rest of the flashy fleet markings so dear to the heart of modellers everywhere, are being diminished in size and reduced to shades of gray.

Naval Aircraft Markings

Each carrier aircraft carries a modex, a three-digit number stencilled on either side of its nose. The first number of the modex denotes the squadron. The wing's two fighter squadrons are given 100 and 200 series modexes. The 300 and 400 series is reserved for the A-7s of the wing's two light attack squadrons. The Hornets will probably wear 300 and 400 modexes when they come into the fleet, except on the older carriers, where they will inherit the fighter role, and the 100 and 200 modexes of the fighter squadrons, from the venerable F-4.

The wing's Intruders wear the 500 series modex of the medium attack squadron. So do the wing's KA-6 tankers. The EA-6s and E-2s carry the 600 series modex. The wing's antisubmarine forces—S-3s and SH-3s—wear the 700 series. Training squadrons carry an 800 series modex.

The modexes were once related to colors used to trim the squadron aircraft. The trim codes were never followed consistently throughout the fleet—tradition took precedence even when the squadron was transferred to another wing. At any rate, all colors are currently disappearing from carrier aircraft (see "Navy Camouflage" appendix). If the planes carry any trim now, it's likely to be a washed-out version of the former color, barely distinguishable in flight. But for history's sake, here are the modexes/trim colors: 100/red, 200/yellow, 300/blue, 400/orange, 500/green, 600 and 700/black.

The other two numbers correspond to specific squadron aircraft. By Navy custom, the first aircraft in the squadron (modex X00, called "double nuts") is reserved for the carrier of the air wing. Called the "CAG Bird" (because the CVW commander was formerly called "Commander, Air Group") it features special trim, commonly stars or stripes, in the colors of the various squadrons in the air wing. Less widespread is the custom of reserving modex X01 for the squadron CO and modex X02 for the squadron XO.

F-14 lines up on Cat 3.

Note that even though these particular aircraft may be marked on the canopy rails with the names and rank of the specific officers, any pilot can and does fly them on a regular basis. In fact, the Navy's Vietnam war ace, Lt. Randall ("Duke") Cunningham, was flying *Constellation's* CAG bird when he made his final three kills.

The codex is a two-digit number that repeats the last two numbers of the modex. The codex is put high on the tail to aid the air boss and the deck handlers in sorting out closely packed aircraft when the modex is not readily distinguishable.

The air boss and the rest of the carrier crew use modexes to sort the aircraft, since the number carried on each plane is unique to the air wing. Sometimes they are even used for call signs, but a more widespread practice is to use the squadron's call sign and the codex.

The tails of Navy aircraft also carry an air wing code. This specific two-letter code corresponds to the carrier to which the wing is currently assigned. Air wings based on the Atlantic coast carry codes beginning with an "A." West Coast air wings' codes begin with an "N" and land-based ASW patrol squadrons have a tail code beginning with "P."

The system is similar to Air Force tail codes, but where USAF birds display the last three digits of their serial number beneath the two-letter codes, Navy air-craft carry a "buno," or bureau number, underneath the horizontal tail. The buno is assigned to each Navy aircraft in sequence of procurement. The "Bureau" referred to, the Bureau of Aeronautics, has since become the Naval Air Systems Command.

In addition, each aircraft carries both the name of the carrier upon which it is currently deployed and its squadron designation stencilled on its fuselage. In the Navy, "V" means fixed wing. The letter is combined with others to denote a particular type of squadron. For example, "VF-XX" is a Navy fixed wing fighter squadron, often referred to as "FITRON XX" or sometimes "Fighting XX."

Some fighter squadrons also carry a "Langley Stripe," a band of color on either side of the canopy that reflects the squadron's tail marking motif. Its origin is unclear, but it seems to distinguish the Navy's original fighter squadrons. Some planes also carry a "battle E." This marking, usually carried on the port side of the canopy or intake, denotes a superior record for a type of squadron in a command—the best fighter squadron in the Atlantic Fleet, for example. Battle S's are similar, celebrating a superior safety record. An excellence letter with hashmarks signifies consecutive awards.

Appendix VII

The Soviet Navy

Warships of the Soviet Navy

This is a book about the U.S. Navy, but this listing of the Soviet Navy's ships was too good to pass up. Often, the Soviet Navy is presented as a floating monolith, but their ships have names, too. Good ones. LCMR Charles E. Adams and noted naval authority Arthur David Baker III performed a needed service by digging up the English equivalents of Russian ships' names. Their list was printed in the Naval Institute *Proceedings* in July 1979. I've added later ones, with translations when available.

Kremlin Class Aircraft Carrier
Kreml   Kremlin

Kiev Class Aircraft Carriers
Kiev   Ukranian city
Minsk   White Russian city
Novorossiysk   Black Sea port city
Kharkov   East Russian city

Moskva Class Helicopter Cruisers
Moskva   Soviet capital
Leningrad   Baltic Sea port

Kirov Class Battle Cruisers
Kirov   Ukrainian city
Frunze   Mikhail Vassilyevich Frunze, former Commander-in-Chief, Soviet Armed Forces

Slava Class Cruiser
Slava   Strength

Kresta I Class Cruisers
Admiral Zozulya   Former Head of Naval Staff
Vladivostok   Sea of Japan city
Vitse Admiral Drozd   WW II naval hero
Sevastopol   Black Sea port city

Kresta II Class Guided Missile Cruisers

Kronshtadt	Baltic port city
Admiral Isakov	Head of Naval Staff, WW II
Admiral Nakhimov	Hero of Russo-Turkish War of 1827
Admiral Makarov	Nineteenth century naval figure
Marshal Voroshilov	WW II Army Commander-in-Chief
Admiral Oktyabr'skiy	Black Sea Fleet Commander, WW II
Admiral Isachenkov	Naval engineer
Marshal Timoshenko	Chairman, Army General Staff, WW II
Vasily Chapaev	Revolutionary and WW II military hero
Admiral Yumashev	WW II Pacific Fleet Commander

Kynda Class Guided Missile Cruisers

Admiral Fokin	WW II Pacific Fleet Commander
Admiral Golovko	WW II Northern Fleet Commander
Groznyy	"Terrible" (Czar Ivan the Terrible)
Varyag	Norseman

Kara Class Guided Missile Cruisers

Nikolaev	Black Sea port city
Ochakov	Black Sea port city
Kerch	Black Sea port city
Azov	Sea of Azov city
Petropavlovsk	Northern Kazakhstan city
Tashkent	Uzbek city
Tallinn	Estonian city

Sovremennyy Class Guided Missile Destroyers

Sovremennyy	Modern
Otchayannyy	
Otlichnyy	

Udaloy Class Guided Missile Destroyers

Udaloy	Courageous
Vitse Admiral Kulakov	WW II Naval Commander
Marshal Vasilevskiy	WW II Army Commander
Admiral Zakharov	Soviet Naval figure

Kashin Class Guided Missile Destroyers

Komsomolets Ukrainy	Ukranian Young Communist
Krasnyy Kavkaz	Red Caucasus
Krasnyy Krym	Red Crimea
Obraztsovyy	Exemplary
Odaryennyy	Gifted
Ognevoy	Burning
Otvazhnyy	Valorous

Provornyy	Swift
Reshitel'nyy	Resolute
Sderzhannyy	Discreet
Skoryy	Speedy
Slavnyy	Famous
Smelyy	Audacious
Smetlivyy	Sharp-witted
Smyshlyennyy	Clever
Soobrazitel'nyy	Quick-witted
Sposobnyy	Capable
Steregushchiy	Watchful
Strogiy	Severe
Stroynyy	Gracious

Kanin Class Guided Missile Destroyers

Boykiy	Smart
Derzkiy	Daring
Gnevnyy	Wrathful
Gordyy	Proud
Gremyashchiy	Thunderous
Upornyy	Tenacious
Zhguchiy	Intense
Zorkiy	Alert

Kildin Class Destroyers

Bedovyy	Mischievous
Neuderzhimyy	Irrepressible
Neulovimyy	Elusive
Prozorlivyy	Sagacious

Kotlin Class Destroyers

Blagorodnyy	Honorable
Blestyashchiy	Brilliant
Bravyy	Gallant
Burlivyy	Tempestuous
Byvalyy	Experienced
Dal'nevostochnyy Komsomolets	Far East Young Communist
Moskovskiy Komsomolets	Moscow Young Communist
Nakhadchivyy	Resourceful
Naporistyy	Assertive
Nastoychivyy	Persistent
Nesokrushimyy	Indestructible
Plamennyy	Ardent
Skromnyy	Modest

Soviet *Alpha* class torpedo attack submarine.

A Soviet Yankee class strategic missile submarine takes up station on patrol. Recent espionage scandals in the U.S. Navy may have seriously jeopardized American ASW secrets.

Skrytnyy	Secretive
Soznatel'nyy	Conscientious
Speshnyy	Urgent
Spokoynyy	Tranquil
Svedushchiy	Experienced
Svetlyy	Lucid
Veskiy	Weighty
Vdoknovennyy	Inspired
Vliyatel'nyy	Influential
Vozbuzhdyennyy	Excited
Vozmushchyennyy	Indignant
Vyderzhannyy	Steadfast
Vyzyvayushchiy	Defiant

Skoryy Class Destroyers

Bessmennyy	Permanent
Besstrashnyy	Fearless
Bezuderzhnyy	Impetuous
Buynyy	Violent
Ognennyy	Fiery
Okrylennyy	Inspired
Ostorozhnyy	Wary
Ostryy	Keen
Otchayannyy	Desperate
Otchyetlivyy	Distinct
Otmennyy	Exquisite
Otvetstvennyy	Responsible

Ozhestochyennyy	Violent
Ozhivlyennyy	Animated
Serdityy	Angry
Ser'yeznyy	Earnest
Smotryashchiy	Sharp-sighted
Sokrushitel'nyy	Shattering
Solidnyy	Strong
Sovershennyy	Perfect
Statnyy	Stately
Stepennyy	Sedate
Stoykiy	Hardy
Stremitel'nyy	Impetuous
Surovyy	Stern
Svobodnyy	Free
Vdumchivyy	Thoughtful
Vnezapnyy	Surprising
Vnimatel'nyy	Attentive
Vol'nyy	Free
Vrazumitel'nyy	Convincing

Krivak I Guided Missile Frigates

Bditel-nyy	Vigilant
Bodryy	Cheerful
Deyatel'nyy	Active
Doblestnyy	Valiant
Dostoynyy	Worthy
Druzhnyy	Harmonious
Leningradskiy Komsomolets	Leningrad Young Communist
Letushiy	Volatile
Razumny	Reasonable
Razyashchiy	Combative
Retivyy	Zealous
Sil'nyy	Powerful
Storozhevoy	Watchful
Svirepyy	Ferocious
Zharkyy	Ardent

Krivak II Guided Missile Frigates

Gromkiy	Celebrated
Grozyashchiy	Threatening
Neukrotimyy	Indomitable
Pylkiy	Ardent
Razitel'nyy	Impressive
Rezkiy	Harsh
Rezvyy	Frisky

Soviet Fleets

Soviet naval bases are widely separated and poorly placed. The numbers of units estimated to be stationed at each base vary, but this Defense Department list is as good a guess as any. The Soviet Navy has also taken up semi-permanent residence in the American-built port of Cam Rahn Bay in Vietnam.

Soviet Red Banner Northern Fleet
HQ: Severomorsk
Bases: Motovsky Gulf,
   Severodvinsk, Polyarny
Warships: 149
Submarines: 151
Auxiliaries: 205
Aircraft: 425

Soviet Red Banner Baltic Fleet
HQ: Kalingrad
Bases: Kronstadt, Talinn,
   Liepaya, Riga
Warships: 141
Submarines: 32
Auxiliaries: 160
Aircraft: 275

Soviet Black Sea Fleet
(Caspian Sea Flotilla)
HQ (Black Sea Fleet): Sevastopol
HQ (Caspian Sea Flotilla): Baku
Bases: Balaklava, Odessa,
   Nikolayev, Tuapse, Poti

Warships: 162
Submarines: 24
Auxiliaries: 180
Aircraft: 405

Soviet Pacific Fleet
HQ: Vladivostok
Bases: Sovietskya Gavan,
   Komsomolsk, Petropavlosk,
   Magadan
Warships: 89
Submarines: 102
Auxiliaries: 235
Aircraft: 440

Mediterranean Squadron (SOVMEDRON)
Major Ports of Call: Tartus,
   Syria; Benghazi, Libya
Warships: 12
Submarines: 12
Auxiliaries: 20

Indian Ocean Squadron (SOVINDRON)
Major Ports of Call: Socotra,
   Democratic Yemen; Dahlak,
   Ethiopia; Seychelles; Beira,
   Mozambique; Mauritus; Sri
   Lanka; India
Warships: 6
Submarines: 1
Auxiliaries: 12

Photo credit: Ian Rutan

Michael Skinner has been a writer and editor for the *St. Petersburg Times, the Washington Star,* and the Cable News Network in Atlanta, Georgia. He is the author of USAFE: A PRIMER OF MODERN AIR COMBAT IN EUROPE and RED FLAG: AIR COMBAT FOR THE '80s (Presidio AIRPOWER books). Skinner is currently at work on a book on USAREUR, the United States Army in Europe.